Searching *for* Lost Ancestors

A Guide to Genealogical Research

Donald E. Underwood
&
Betty A. Underwood

FITHIAN PRESS
SANTA BARBARA
1993

*To all of our relatives, dead or alive,
who made this book possible.*

Printed in the United States of America

The authors gratefully acknowledge permission to reprint in this book illustrations supplied by the following: The Everton Publishers, *G.A.S. Lites* (a publication of the Genealogical Association of Sacramento), the Sutro Library, the U.S. National Archives and Records Administration, Valley Software, and Hurdware, Inc.

Design and typography by Jim Cook

Published by Fithian Press
Post Office Box 1525
Santa Barbara, California 93102

LIBRARY OF CONGRESS CATALOGING-IN-PUBLICATION DATA
Underwood, Donald E.
Searching for lost ancestors: a guide to genealogical research / Donald E. and Betty A. Underwood.
p. cm.
Includes bibliographical references and index.
ISBN 1-56474-040-4
1. Genealogy 2. United States–Genealogy–Handbooks, manuals, etc.
I. Underwood, Betty A. II. Title.
CS16.U47 1993
929'.1'072073—dc 20 92-28835
CIP

Contents

List of Figures

Introduction

> Not to know what has been transacted in former times is to be always a child. If no use is made of the labors of past ages, the world must remain always in the infancy of knowledge.
>
> —CICERO

What were they like, those ancestors of ours? Why did they leave their native land to come to this country? What particular quality did they possess that motivated them to leave everything familiar and safe to venture forth to this new alien land? Do I inherit any of these qualities and attributes from them?

Genealogical research cannot answer all of these questions: it can only fill some of the blanks for you. Whether they were saints or sinners, persons of property or hard-working farmers, all have one thing in common: they are all your ancestors, and that makes them special to you in a way that no one else can claim.

It is this interpersonal relationship that genealogy is most concerned with, and it is what differentiates genealogy from the other branches of history. But genealogy and history cannot be separated; people are part and parcel of the times and places they occupy in this universe. All of the events that have contributed to the shaping and development of countries have also had a profound impact upon the destinies of our own early forebears. Wars, political upheavals, famines, and epidemics were among the many factors that determined not only the migration routes and settlement locations of the early travelers to our shores, but also many of the past movements of the emigrants within the borders of the young United States.

In researching your early ancestors you will read accounts of Indian raids on small settlements and of major battles fought at places familiar to us through our history books. Throughout the historical narrative there will be one main recurring theme, that of your own personal history unfolding before you as you delve back into the past, diligently pursuing each piece of information your research uncovers.

You will meet ancestors you never knew about and be reacquainted with family legends of which you may have heard in great detail. As your research progresses, all of these shadowy figures will slowly but surely emerge into the light of this present century. For genealogical research is much like working a giant jigsaw puzzle; most of the pieces are there, if you can only find them. Every part of the puzzle you uncover adds a little to the overall configuration, slowly forming before your eyes.

As the picture starts to grow, you will become more and more involved with these strangers who are so tied in with your own destiny. What if a certain chance meeting between two of your ancestors had never occurred? Perhaps they might never have met and married, thus discontinuing the direct line that led to you. Would you be here today anyway? The thought is sobering. It has been said that all life and death is based on accidents, and although there can be no definite answer to that statement, we are all aware of the role that chance plays in our existence. And that may be one of the reasons that genealogical research is so important to us, allowing us to see, retrospectively, the unfolding drama of our own personal history.

Part One
FINDING AND RESEARCHING THE RECORDS

CHAPTER 1

Beginning the Search

> It is indeed a desirable thing to be well descended,
> but the glory belongs to our ancestors.
>
> —PLUTARCH

It is sometimes difficult to remember just exactly when you began to speculate about your long-dead kin. Small things can suddenly bring to mind an older relative's comments regarding some remote ancestor. Did Great Aunt Jennie really have fifteen cats? Did we really have an ancestor who was a court painter in England, as mother so often claimed? It makes a great story, but, you say to yourself, "Someday I am going to really check that one out." Maybe that is one of the reasons why it suddenly becomes so urgent for you to start investigating your own personal detective story. Or perhaps there is another reason. It is conceivable that we become more interested in our family history when we become aware that we, and our families, are steadily adding to it. The pattern continues and the concentric circle grows as our own personal statistics are added for future generations to speculate upon.

Whatever your motivating reason, questions which may immediately present themselves to you might be, "But where do I start and how do I begin? What is the first thing that I must do?" To be suddenly confronted with such an ambitious undertaking can be intimidating to some, especially if one is a neophyte genealogist.

However, the answer to these questions is a simple one. You start with yourself.

Begin by writing down everything you know about yourself, using every source and all of the information that is available to you. Generally you will find that the best place to start your research is right in your own home, where most of your personal records are usually kept.

At this stage, one point cannot be stressed too strongly. Careful beginning documentation is crucial for your later research. When you start investigating the many outside sources that are available, you will frequently find names similar to the one you are researching. Thus you will need all of the available information you can extract ahead of time in order to ascertain proper ancestor identification. Do not omit anything, since the smallest detail can sometimes turn out to be noteworthy for your later research.

There are many excellent documented sources of genealogical information to be found at home, and one of the most important is the family Bible—either yours or a relative's, or better still, both. Before vital statistics were required to be maintained by the states, the family Bible was sometimes the only place a birth, death, marriage, or any other event important to the family was recorded. If the birth or death were fairly recent, then official vital records might be obtained from the state or county of occurrence. These official records can be very revealing, sometimes indicating the parents of the individual, where they were from, and occasionally, the father's occupation.

Other home sources to check are old letters, official birth and death certificates, old family albums, wills, deeds, and even old newspaper clippings or obituaries. Again, remember to write down everything you find, for even a middle initial can make a difference in an identification. Or the fact that your great grandfather was born in New Jersey, not in Ohio, as you had thought, can sometimes open new doors for your research. Sometimes wedding books and baby books can indicate important dates in the family history. Also, family account books of business transactions can reveal property transfers or sales of important holdings to other relatives or family connections.

After you have investigated and documented as much home source material as you can find, your next step should be personal interviews with your immediate family relatives. Start with those most convenient, either at home or nearby, graduating at a later date to the more far-flung relatives, contacting them by telephone, letter, or by a personal visit. Interviewing the oldest ones first is a good way to start. Try to find out from your grandparents, for example, everything they know about their own parents and grandparents, such as names, dates, and places of birth, and anything else they can recall. Try to document everything they say, exactly as it is related to you. Later evidence might clarify any ambiguous facts.

After interviewing local relatives, it might be expedient to correspond with, or plan a visit to, your out-of-town relatives. You might even encounter one who has done a little research on his own. It certainly would be a boon to both of you if you could exchange notes, each supplying invaluable family information to the other. Some out-of-town relatives, especially the elderly, might even possess old family papers or records that could reveal much of genealogical value. It is possible that, until you contact them, they might not even realize what they have, so it is to your advantage to explore all possibilities.

In documenting all this information, try to find out from your sources exactly when and where your ancestors lived and with whom. It is important to determine relationships, if you can, for later identification or clarification. Also, determining your ancestor's occupation can be valuable for research purposes. Information regarding brothers and sisters of your direct line is especially important in genealogical research. Frequently, family member names are the only means of identification of an early ancestor when a similar name is seen in an official document. They are also important as input toward your own completed pedigree or ancestry record.

If you are looking for information in an area where you have no living relatives, genealogical magazines are an excellent source of information. For a fee, you can advertise for information in your area of interest regarding any surname you are researching. Any answers will be sent directly to you for your action. One such publication, *The Genealogical Helper* (Everton Publishers, Inc., P.O. Box 368, Logan, Utah, 84321), specializes in this service. It also provides information about many other genealogical points of interest such as lists of historical societies and libraries.

While we're on the subject of names, try to find out if your ancestors used more than one spelling of the family surname. Even the most common name frequently started out as something completely different. Surnames have been changed throughout history for many different reasons. Sometimes a surname was changed deliberately for reasons of expediency by its possessor, sometimes because of a careless rendition by the ancestor, or occasionally, because of a misinterpretation of the spelling by others. Whatever your name, do not be surprised to find it spelled in many different ways, especially the further back you go in your research. You might even find out that your original immigrant ancestor came from a completely different part of the world and was of a completely different national origin than you had always been led to believe. Such are the surprises genealogical research can hold for you.

- *Personal Records*
Family Bibles
Oral traditions
Journals and diaries
Letters
Scrapbooks
Photographs
Farm records
Health and medical records
Citizenship papers
Social Security cards
Employment records
- *Certificates*
Birth
Marriage
Death
Adoption
Baptism
Confirmation
Manumission
Divorce
- *School Records*
Elementary
Secondary
Vocational
Trade
College
University
Private
- *Insurance Records*
Life
Fire
Automobile
Accident
Health
- *Vital Records*
Birth
Death Marriage
Divorce
Adoption
- *Marriage Records*
Indexes
Banns
Bonds
Licenses
Contracts
- *Genealogical Society of Utah*
Family group records
Intl. Genealogical Index
Ancestral File
Family Register
- *Printed Sources*
Family histories
Genealogies
Biographies
Pedigrees
Local histories
City directories
- *Genealogical Periodicals*
Indexes
Queries
Genealogies
- *U.S. Census Records*
Indexes
1790 1850
1800 1860
1810 1870
1820 1880
1830 1900
1840 1910
- *Mortality Records*
- *State Census*
- *Local Census*
- *Land Records*
Grantee index
Grantor indexes
Deeds
Mortgages
Patents
Grants
- *Probate Records*
Indexes
Wills
Bonds
Guardianships
- *Tax Records*
Personal property
Real estate
- *Military Records*
Service files
Pensions
Bounty awards
Discharges
- *Immigration Records*
Passenger lists
Passports
Oaths of allegiance
Naturalization
Custom records
- *Cemetery Records*
Monuments
Plats
Deeds
Tombstones
- *Church Records*
Birth
Christening
Baptism
Marriage
Banns
Divorce
Death
Burial
Removals
Membership lists
- *Newspapers*
Indexes
Births
Deaths
Marriages
Obituaries

Figure 1: Source Checklist

Chapter 2

Your Record System

> Out of monuments, names, words, proverbs, traditions, private records and evidences, fragments of stories, passages of books, and the like, we do save and recover somewhat from the deluge of time.
>
> —Francis Bacon

When you have researched all of the available records in and around your home and have amassed as much information that is on hand, you may find that you have quite an accumulation of names, places and dates, as well as many other various and sundry bits and pieces of family history. The question is now, what to do with it? At this point in your research, it is important to start organizing and documenting the data collected. This will give an overall view of what information you actually have and, in turn, can help ascertain just what other information you will need for your completed ancestry chart.

But, a word of caution before you proceed. Genealogy, as well as its sister subject, history, is only as valid as accurate recording and careful documentation can make it. Stories of colorful, dashing ancestors and romantic family legends as handed down from generation to generation are a lot of fun to listen to and pass on. However, unless proven valid by correlating information found in more official sources, it is best to treat these tales as romantic fiction and not document them as part of your pedigree. If you want these stories remembered, write the pertinent data in pencil, marked with a check, to indicate its invalidated status. Also, and this bears repeating, any other uncorrelated data should always be listed in pencil, and this includes the dates and names on your ancestral charts, or pedigree forms, as they were once called. Occasionally when questioning elderly relatives, their memories play tricks, and facts and figures can vary from interview to interview. In the event the names and dates are officially verified later, they can always be inked in at that time, saving recopying the original figures.

This does not mean that you should skip conversations with your elderly relatives. Quite the contrary. One of the most intriguing and occasionally critical aspects of ancestor searching can be the interviews with, for example, your Great-aunt Maude, who may have outlived most of her own generation, or garrulous old Uncle Abe who reminisces at great length with the slightest encouragement. Some old people have surprisingly accurate memories and can readily supply you with exactly the right information; it is just a matter of asking the right ones.

As we indicated in Chapter 1, if your grandparents are still alive, you should start with them. Whether you do your interviewing in person, by mail, or by way of a third party, it is important that you utilize the proper forms. Copies of your ancestry charts and the family group records would be helpful to bring along or send to serve as memory aids. Be sure to also carry a separate notebook for posting any enlightening family anecdotes or stories that you may be able to incorporate later into your family history.

Basically, you will need to start with two 8½ x 11 loose-leaf notebooks. One notebook will contain your basic family history forms, such as the ancestry charts and the family group records. The other notebook can be used to transcribe not only the personal narratives of your elderly relatives, but also valuable abstracted data you will obtain later from census records, wills, deeds, bibles, and vital records, to name a few.

It would be beneficial to include in your information notebook a personal data sheet for each individual you are researching. If you list the facts in chronological order, you will find that, in the future, writing a biographical sketch or constructing a genealogy will be much simpler for you. Be sure, however, to always document your sources for each separate entry in your ledger. It would be wise to immediately set up a special family surname source information file that will grow as your research continues.

If you plan to interview your relative in person, a tape recorder would be a very useful tool. However, a note of caution regarding the use of tape recorders; sometimes knowing a conversation is being recorded can be intimidating to an interviewee. There is always a possibility you may be inadvertently rattling a family skeleton or stirring up a painful memory, so be sure you always ask permission before you turn it on. And while you are recording their answers, it is well to also take notes for clarification of their responses later, if necessary. Sometimes you may not get a second chance to interview an elderly relative.

It is best to always know what specific information you will need from a particular relative. Your ancestry chart and family group records will indicate by their blank spaces just what data you are lacking, so be sure to give copies to your relatives for their input. Be ready to supply them with blank forms for their ancestral records, too, if needed. Whenever you add data to your charts or note an interesting anecdote for your history record, it is important to indicate the time, date, place, and person interviewed.

There are some important rules to remember when filling out the ancestry forms. Names should always be completely spelled out. Dates should always be indicated in order of the day, month, and year without numbering the month, as in 12 May, 1820. Remember always to record the information as is. If there is a discrepancy with earlier data, place a small pencil check mark beside the new information as a notation for future research.

In the case of deceased relatives, document the date of death and cemetery where buried, if known. Sometimes you will find that a departed ancestor may not be buried in the same locale where he died. If the cemetery is not indicated, futile time may be wasted trying to research all of the graveyards in the wrong area. Death dates and places are extremely valuable for research purposes, as a certificate of death can yield much extra information. If your ancestor died before death certificates were required by federal or state law, then you may have to check church, cemetery, and funeral home records.

At any rate, the first of the charts to be filled in is the ancestral chart, or pedigree form as it was formerly called, which covers direct line ancestors only. It is a quick and handy reference guide for you as it tells at a glance just where you are in your research. There are several forms you can use including those that cover four and six generations and some that cover as many as ten generations (see a five generation chart, Figure 2).

You begin documenting your ancestral chart by listing a number 1 at the top of the form as this is your record and this is always your own number. You are also number 1 on the very first line to the left on which you start by posting your full name, spelling out any initials. Under your name, you list your date of birth, putting the day first, spelling out the month, with the year last. Under this, you list your place of birth, and below that your marriage date, if applicable.

Again, remember not to abbreviate if a full name is known. Some people like to capitalize a surname, follow by a comma, and post the given name last. Others list the names in their natural order; it is really a matter of preferences of whatever works for you.

The next two horizontal lines to your left indicate your paternal and maternal lines. On the upper of these parallel lines, write your father's number which is 2, and his full name. Under his name, write his date and place of birth, his marriage date, and death date, if deceased. In the case of dead relatives, if the funeral home is known, document this also; this information can be useful later.

Next of the lower of the two horizontal lines is your mother's line, which is number 3. Document her in the same way as your father with one exception, you list her by her full maiden name only. In order to facilitate research into the maternal lines, women are always indicated by their maiden names, if known.

On the lines following your father's and mother's names, list their parents in the same way, labeling his father number 4, and his mother 5, while her father is number 6, and her mother becomes number 7. You document the same information in a similar fashion of each of them.

The next column over consists of eight lines, four are your father's grandparents and numbered 8 through 11, while four are your mother's grandparents and numbered 12 through 15. On

Date ____________
Name of Compiler D. Underwood
Address ____________
City ____________ State ____________
Person No. 1 on this chart is the same person as No. ______ on chart No. ______

Pedigree Chart No. 1

b. Date of Birth
p.b. Place of Birth
m. Date of Marriage
d. Date of Death
p.d. Place of Death

4 William A. Morse
(Father of No. 2)
b. 8 November 1754
p.b. Salisbury, Massachusetts
m. 6 May 1778
d. 12 February 1811
p.d. Andover, Massachusetts

2 John C. Morse
(Father of No. 1)
b. 23 December 1780
p.b. Andover, Massachusetts
m. 5 July 1800
d. 18 March 1848
p.d. Wilton, Maine

5 Betsy L. Sawyer
(Mother of No. 2)
b. 17 August 1755
p.b. Salem, Massachusetts
d. 2 February 1806
p.d. Andover, Massachusetts

1 John C. Morse Jr.
b. 14 October 1806
p.b. Wilton, Maine
m. 14 November 1827
d. 12 May 1871
p.d. St. Louis

6 Samuel E. Matthews
(Father of No. 3)
b. 21 August 1753
p.b. Ipswich, Massachusetts
m. 28 April 1778
d. 19 February 1811
p.d. Wilton, Maine

3 Abigail S. Matthews
(Mother of No. 1)
b. 17 May 1781
p.b. Ipswich, Massachusetts
d. 16 October 1845
p.d. Wilton, Maine

7 Jenny L. Barton
(Mother of No. 3)
b. 9 September 1760
p.b. Rowley, Massachusetts
d. 12 April 1831
p.d. Wilton. Maine

Esther L. Abbot
(Husband or Wife of No. 1)
b. 3 June 1808
p.b. Bangor, Maine
d. 8 March 1877
p.d. St. Louis, Missouri

The Everton Publishers, Box 368, Logan, Utah 84321, For F-5

Figure 2: Pedigree Chart No. 1
(Reprinted by permission of The Everton Publishers, Inc., Logan Utah)

8 Thomas E. Morse
(Father of No. 4)
b. 4 May 1732
p.b. Methuen, Massachusetts
m. 30 April 1753
d. 11 December 1798
p.d. Salisbury, Massachusetts

9 Sarah C. Thomas
(Mother of No. 4)
b. 2 November 1735
p.b. Methuen, Massachusetts
d. 12 May 1789
p.d. Salisbury, Massachusetts

10 James J. Sawyer
(Father of No. 5)
b. 22 April 1732
p.b. Salem, Massachusetts
m. 28 May 1752
d. 19 June 1771
p.d. Methuen, Massachusetts

11 Nancy Miller
(Mother of No. 5)
b. 16 June 1734
p.b. Boston, Massachusetts
d. 23 November 1789
p.d. Methuen, Massachusetts

12 John Matthews
(Father of No. 6)
b. 22 July 1725
p.b. Ipswich, Massachusetts
m. 17 June 1752
d. 11 November 1796
p.d. Ipswich, Massachusetts

13 Susan C. Arnold
(Mother of No. 6)
b. 4 April 1727
p.b. Salisbury, Massachusetts
d. 16 May 1786
p.d. Ipswich, Massachusetts

14 Preston A. Barton
(Father of No. 7)
b. 2 May 1729
p.b. Rowley, Massachusetts
m. 14 October 1748
d. 29 June 1789
p.d. Rowley, Massachusetts

15 Hannah Dimmock
(Mother of No. 7)
b. 6 March 1731
p.b. Newbury, Massachusetts
d. 26 November 1782
p.d. Rowley, Massachusetts

16 William H. Morse
(Father of No. 8)
Continued on chart 2

17 Elizabeth Williams
(Mother of No. 8)
Continued on chart 3

18 Jonathan Thomas
(Father of No. 9)
Continued on chart 4

19 Sarah Mathes
(Mother of No. 9)
Continued on chart 5

20 Henry R. Sawyer
(Father of No. 10)
Continued on chart 6

21 Jane Hinds
(Mother of No. 10)
Continued on chart 7

22 George Miller
(Father of No. 11)
Continued on chart 8

23 Martha Green
(Mother of No. 11)
Continued on chart 9

24 Edward Matthews
(Father of No. 12)
Continued on chart 10

25 Mary Gibson
(Mother of No. 12)
Continued on chart 11

26 Gilbert Arnold
(Father of No. 13)
Continued on chart 12

27 Susanna Wyeth
(Mother of No. 13)
Continued on chart 13

28 Philip T. Barton
(Father of No. 14)
Continued on chart 14

29 Martha Groves
(Mother of No. 14)
Continued on chart 15

30 Stephen Dimmock
(Father of No. 15)
Continued on chart 16

31 Hannah Simpson
(Mother of No. 15)
Continued on chart 17

these, your great-grandparents' lines, their vital statistics are recorded in the same way. Remember to post in pencil any data not verified yet.

The remaining sixteen lines belong to your fifth-generation ancestors and are posted only with the appropriate forebear's name and sequentially numbered. Each fifth-generation ancestor can be extended onto his own individual chart where he or she will become a first generation number 1, but with a different chart number (see Figure 3).

In Figure 3, you will note that whichever fifth-generation ancestor you are documenting will become number 1, or the first generation on his own pedigree chart. His chart number, however, will be whatever number he was assigned on your ancestry chart. Although other numbering methods are sometimes used, this method of reassignment of numbers allows you to extend back in your history as far as you will probably be able to go and the numbering system should be easy to follow.

The next form of importance to your family history is one called the family group record (see Figure 4). As the ancestry chart deals with direct lines only, a system for documenting the other family members is needed and this record is the answer. It reveals such important information as the birth, death, marriages, and occupation of the direct line ancestor and his offspring. Any unusual information concerning a family member, such as a nickname, if any, whether adopted or a twin, and sometimes his religion, useful for church research purposes, can be posted on this one-page record.

A family group record should be filled out for every direct line ancestor on your ancestry chart and for all of your siblings. If a sibling is married, he (or she) will also need his own family group record. As you can see, you will need a great many of these family records, as every direct line ancestor, or sibling who was married more than once will need a separate record for each spouse. If this seems like a great deal of documentation, you will note later that this information will prove valuable for ancestor identification.

Record the information on each person on the family group sheet exactly as you did on the ancestry chart. Each of the children should be posted in the order of birth, recording everything known about the event, such as where and when it occurred.

Particularly important to document is your source of information. This data will become necessary if you need to verify your descent in order to join a patriotic organization or any other society that requires proof of your heredity.

Be sure that in documenting the family group record you list as much information as the form calls for. This is important too, because someday someone might be researching the same line and will need all of the information available.

When you have finished recording your immediate family, do the same for your parents, your grandparents, and your great-grandparents for as far back as you can, listing them each on their own family group record. As indicated before, any information that is not verified should be written in pencil for future corrections, if necessary. Post your sources on the family group sheet and in the surname file for quick cross-referencing.

Although the two above-described ancestry charts are considered the mainstays of a family history program, there are other pedigree forms that some researchers like to utilize for their documentation that offer a different perspective to a family history program. One such pedigree form is called a radial chart and is drawn as a full circle for both the paternal and the maternal lines, or as a semi-circle if only one line is to be shown (see Figure 5). This chart, if filled out fully, has the effect of showing at a glance, your complete ancestral background as far back as the circle has spaces, starting with yourself in the center and working outward to your remotest ancestor. It has the appearance somewhat of a giant sunburst with the rays going off in all directions and the lines getting finer and closer together the further away from the center they go.

These charts and others like them can be purchased in most genealogical bookstores or you can draw your own if you feel ambitious.

Although some of the above-described methods of recording family history are more popular than others, there is no one system that is superior to the rest. The only criteria is what you desire as the end result of this enterprise. But whether your ultimate goal is to publish your full family history, or merely to compile your own genealogy to pass along to an interested family member, you need to know the basic difference between the various approaches.

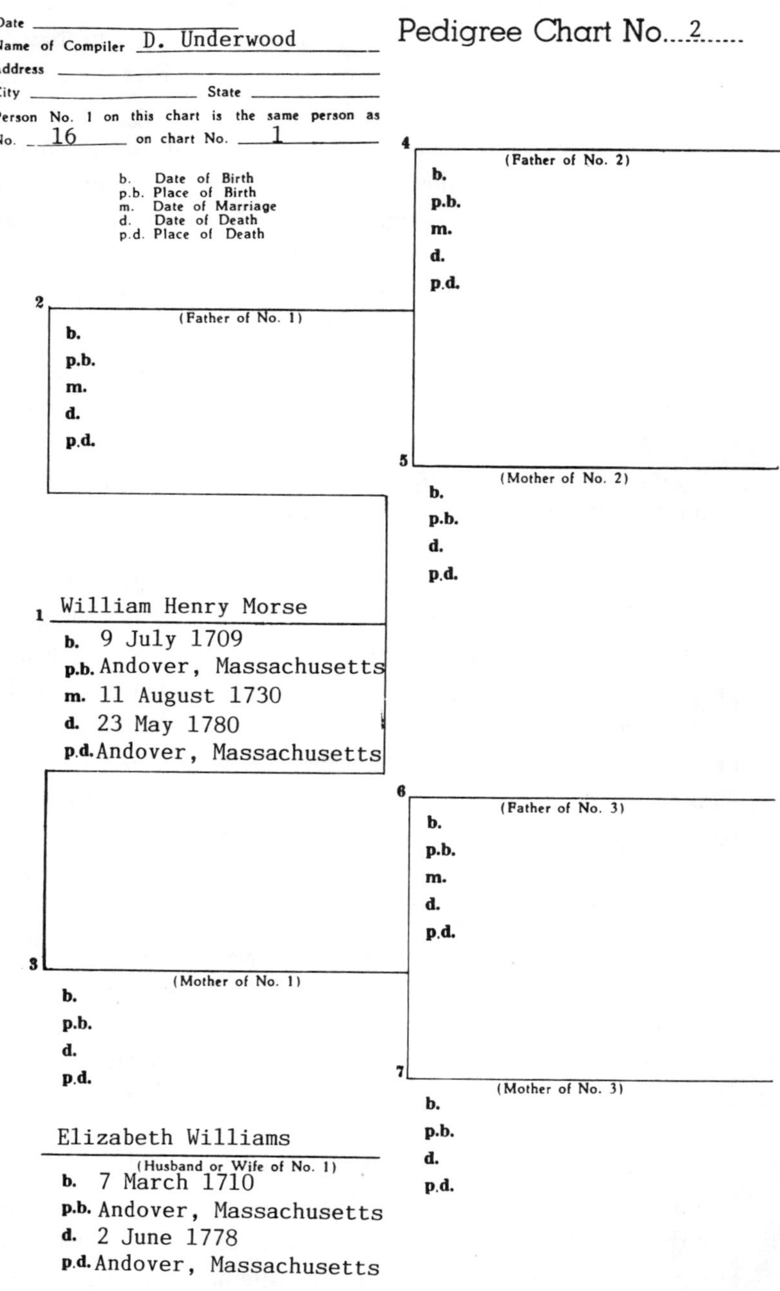

Date
Name of Compiler D. Underwood
Address
City State
Person No. 1 on this chart is the same person as No. 16 on chart No. 1

Pedigree Chart No. 2

b. Date of Birth
p.b. Place of Birth
m. Date of Marriage
d. Date of Death
p.d. Place of Death

4 (Father of No. 2)
b.
p.b.
m.
d.
p.d.

2 (Father of No. 1)
b.
p.b.
m.
d.
p.d.

5 (Mother of No. 2)
b.
p.b.
d.
p.d.

1 William Henry Morse
b. 9 July 1709
p.b. Andover, Massachusetts
m. 11 August 1730
d. 23 May 1780
p.d. Andover, Massachusetts

6 (Father of No. 3)
b.
p.b.
m.
d.
p.d.

3 (Mother of No. 1)
b.
p.b.
d.
p.d.

7 (Mother of No. 3)
b.
p.b.
d.
p.d.

Elizabeth Williams
(Husband or Wife of No. 1)
b. 7 March 1710
p.b. Andover, Massachusetts
d. 2 June 1778
p.d. Andover, Massachusetts

The Everton Publishers, Box 368, Logan, Utah 84321. For F-5

Figure 3: Pedigree Chart No. 2
(Reprinted by permission of The Everton Publishers, Inc., Logan Utah)

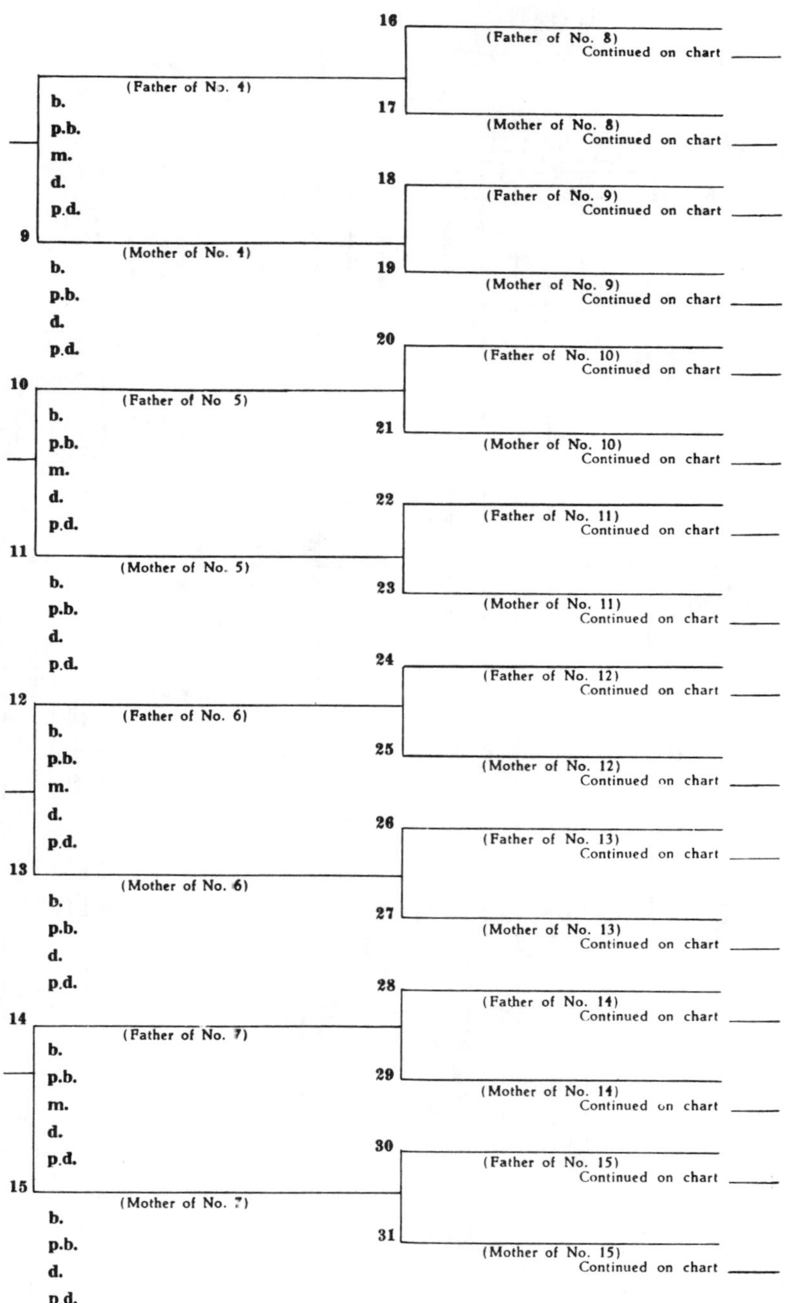
16
(Father of No. 8)
Continued on chart
(Father of No. 4)
b.
17
p.b.
(Mother of No. 8)
Continued on chart
m.
d.
18
p.d.
(Father of No. 9)
Continued on chart
9
(Mother of No. 4)
b.
19
p.b.
(Mother of No. 9)
Continued on chart
d.
p.d.
20
(Father of No. 10)
Continued on chart
10
(Father of No 5)
b.
21
p.b.
(Mother of No. 10)
Continued on chart
m.
d.
22
p.d.
(Father of No. 11)
Continued on chart
11
(Mother of No. 5)
b.
23
p.b.
(Mother of No. 11)
Continued on chart
d.
p.d.
24
(Father of No. 12)
Continued on chart
12
(Father of No. 6)
b.
25
p.b.
(Mother of No. 12)
Continued on chart
m.
d.
26
p.d.
(Father of No. 13)
Continued on chart
13
(Mother of No. 6)
b.
27
p.b.
(Mother of No. 13)
Continued on chart
d.
p.d.
28
(Father of No. 14)
Continued on chart
14
(Father of No. 7)
b.
p.b.
29
(Mother of No. 14)
Continued on chart
m.
d.
30
p.d.
(Father of No. 15)
Continued on chart
15
(Mother of No. 7)
b.
31
p.b.
(Mother of No. 15)
Continued on chart
d.
p.d.

FAMILY GROUP RECORD

ENTER ALL DATA IN THIS ORDER: NAMES: WATSON, John Henry
DATES: 14 Apr 1794 PLACES: Sharon, Windsr, Vt

To indicate that a child is an ancestor of the family representative, place an "X" behind the number pertaining to that child.

HUSBAND (full name)
Born (date) 23 December 1780 Place Andover, Essex, Massachusetts
Chr. (date) Place
Marr. (date) 5 July 1800 Place Ipswich, Essex, Massachusetts
Died (date) 18 March 1848 Place Wilton, Franklin, Maine
Bur. (date) 20 March 1848 Place Wilton, Franklin, Maine
HUSBAND'S FATHER (full name) William Albert Morse HUSBAND'S MOTHER (full maiden name) Betsy Lou Sawyer
HUSBAND'S OTHER WIVES

WIFE (full maiden name) Abigail Sue Matthews
Born (date) 17 May 1781 Place Ipswich, Essex, Massachusetts
Chr. (date) 21 October 1782 Place Ipswich, Essex, Massachusetts
Died (date) 16 October 1845 Place Wilton, Franklin, Maine
Bur. (date) 18 October 1845 Place Wilton, Franklin, Maine
WIFE'S FATHER (full name) Samuel Edward Matthews WIFE'S MOTHER (full maiden name) Jenny Louise Burton
WIFE'S OTHER HUSBANDS

No.	SEX M F	CHILDREN (full names) List Each Child (Whether Living or Dead) in Order of Birth — SURNAME (CAPITALIZED) GIVEN NAMES	WHEN BORN — DAY MONTH YEAR	WHERE BORN — TOWN	COUNTY	STATE OR COUNTRY	DATE OF FIRST MARRIAGE — TO WHOM	WHEN DIED — DAY MONTH YEAR
1	M	Henry Lee Morse	2 September 1801	Andover	Essex	Mass.	9 June 1819 Sally Simpson	12 Aug. 1882
2	M	William Glen Morse	14 November 1804	Andover	Essex	Mass.	17 October 1826 Jane Taylor	7 May 1867
3 X	M	John Cabot Morse Jr.	14 October 1806	Andover	Essex	Mass.	14 November 1827 Esther Abbott	12 May 1871
4	F	Abigail May Morse	24 October 1809	Wilton	Frank.	Maine	3 May 1830 John Mason	6 Nov. 1874
5	M	Samuel M. Morse	18 June 1810	Wilton	Frank.	Maine	14 March 1828 Susan Henry	28 Apr. 1883
6	F	Mary Lou Morse	15 July 1813	Wilton	Frank.	Maine	7 May 1834 Henry Morgan	2 Feb. 1885
7								
8								
9								
10								
11								

SOURCES OF INFORMATION

OTHER MARRIAGES

Figure 4: Family Group Record

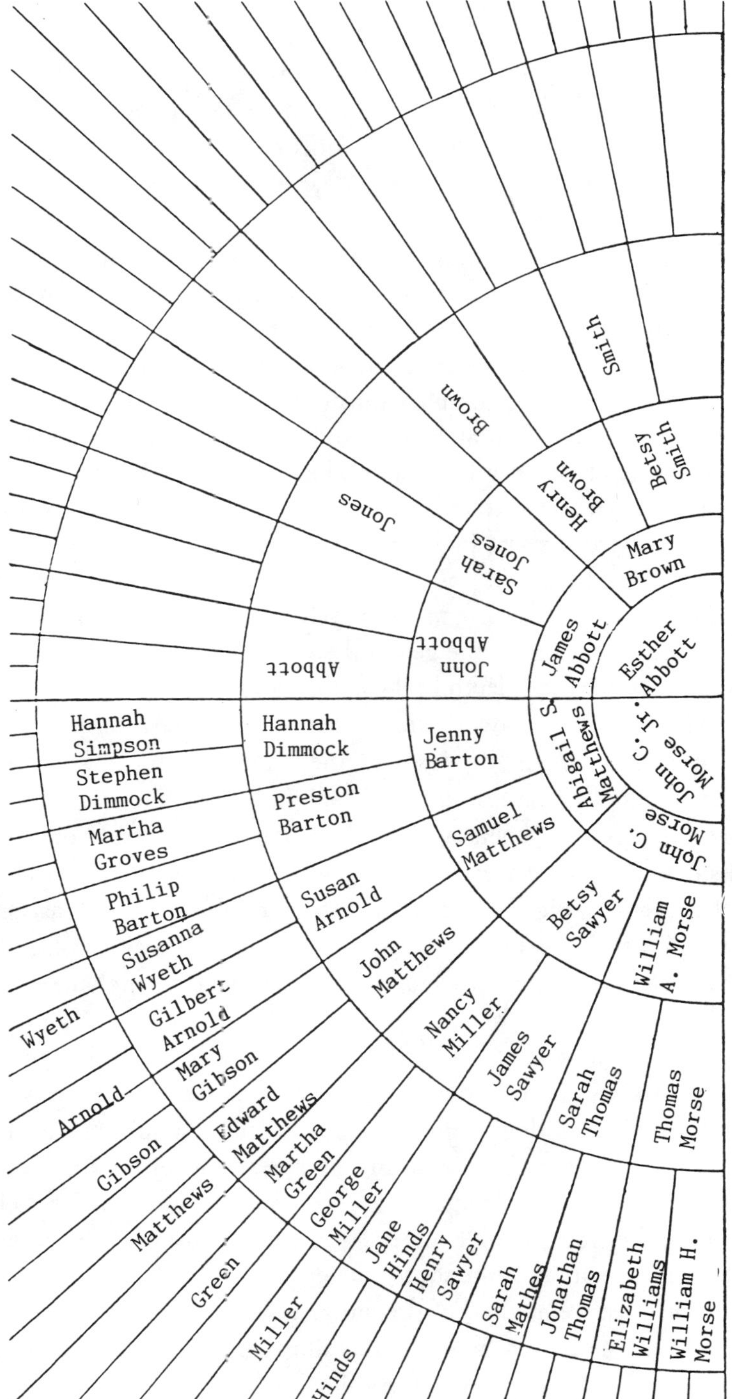

Figure 5: Radial Chart

For example, there is a difference between compiling a family history and arranging a family genealogy. The family historian begins at the end of the line and works back, and the genealogist starts at the beginning and works forward and the end results are, predictably, quite opposite.

A family history is comprised of the ascendants of one individual who is the latest descendant of his line. His ancestry chart begins with himself and works backward to his remotest ancestor, desirably the original immigrant forebear. The hoped-for final result of this endeavor is the complete direct lineage of the individual.

This method of compilation has been referred to by some as personal family history because the historian attempts to concentrate on particular ancestral lines, obtaining, if possible, all of the historical data of every ancestor rather than just the facts of life of marriage, birth, death, and kinship that the genealogist is more concerned with. It is left to the family historian to flesh out the bare facts set down by the genealogist, adding by historical narrative, dimension, and depth to the family chronicle.

The genealogist, on the other hand, completely reverses the method of documentation used by the family historian. He begins with the family's earliest-known immigrant progenitor and traces down by descent, generation by generation to the present one. As this extensive task covers a multitude of individuals, the genealogist must be more conversant with source locations and analysis than with such abstract issues of, for example, the social, political, or economic climates that may have contributed to the ancestor's emigration.

Because his records are frequently used to establish lineage to claim legacies, or to prove descent from a Revolutionary War ancestor, the genealogist must be able to accurately substantiate all matters of kinship or relationship in a neat and orderly fashion. He must not only be concerned with exact identification of each ancestor, but must be able to present these conclusions as based on a logical evaluation of the source material.

One effective method of presenting a genealogy in this fashion is a system, employed by many genealogists and recommended by the New England Historic Genealogical Society. Known as the "Register form," it combines the features of a narrative with a numerical system and has the advantage of presenting the original ancestor's genealogy in a more readable and entertaining fashion than the naked outlines of the ancestry forms can usually provide.

To arrange a genealogy using this method, one begins, as was indicated, with the family's earliest known immigrant ancestor in this country. As the family progenitor, he is assigned the first number, an arabic number (1). Although any numbering system can be utilized, the New England Historic Genealogical Society recommends the use of arabic numbers for heads of families, (1, 2, 3, 4) with lower case roman numerals used to indicate the children in order of their birth, (i, ii, iii). If a child is also a parent with his own family, he (or she) will also be assigned an arabic number in addition to a lower case roman number. For an example, see the following account.

GENERATION 1.

1. JOHN JONES (1630-1699)

Start with the name of the immigrant ancestor or the first known ancestor in America; the dates and places of his birth, death, and burial site. List his parents, their vital statistics, and residence, if known. Indicate his country of origin, how he came to this country, the ship he sailed on, and any other background material you have on him, including the source material for this information.

List his marriage information next, including the date and place, the bride's full name, and her birth and death records. Her parentage should be listed here, also. If she was a widow, or remarried after the ancestor's death, list this along with the name or names of any of her successive husbands. Any unusual circumstances or particulars of her life can be listed here, or, if extensive, at the end of the account.

The next paragraph should tell of the forebear's achievements, education, and accomplishments including his military or civil service and occupation. Any other interesting or unusual details of his life that can add color to his story such as the migratory pattern of his life or any offices he held should be noted here.

In the last paragraph you list his children in chronological order as:

Issue:

i. John Jr., b. (date and place); d. young (date and place).

2. ii. Susan, b. (date and place); d. (date and place); m. husband's name (date and place of birth and death).

3. iii. George, b. (date and place); d. (date and place); wife's name (date and place of birth and death).

How you handle the descent of the children depends upon whether you are doing a family history of only one direct line such as yourself, or a family genealogy of all of the descendants of the original progenitor. If you are concentrating on the direct line to yourself, you assign successive arabic numerals only to those ancestors from whom you descend. If, however, all of the descendants of the original ancestors are listed, each of his children with continuing lines will be assigned his or her own arabic numerals, and their succeeding children designated the lower case numbers as indicated above.

For example, Susan, as next in the continuing generations, is assigned a small roman number (ii) as the second born to John Jones, the family progenitor. However, as the first member of the second generation to continue the line, she is also assigned an arabic (2) to indicate her status as the progenitor of her own line.

At the end of the account, it would be a good idea to list your reference sources. If your reference material came from a book, be sure to list the author's name, book title, and publication date. Other sources, even if personal family records, should be documented carefully, also. You, or someone else, may wish to verify some of the data at a later time, as accuracy is essential.

CHAPTER 3

Additional Recording Practices

> He is wise who knows the sources of knowledge—who knows who has written and where it is to be found.
>
> —A.A. HODGE

As you continue to document the surname you are researching it is a good practice to record everyone with the same surname in the area in which you are working. You might later find new clues leading toward another ancestor in the same locale. A complete surname search the first time around can save you valuable research time. Also, in reevaluating the information you have compiled, occasionally you will find later that the name you almost overlooked led to another line that, until now, you were unaware of. In genealogy, frequently the smallest details can sometimes open new lines of endeavor. You cannot afford to overlook anything that might be relevant to the search, especially when you begin investigating the many outside sources of public and private records that are available to the diligent genealogical researcher.

While we are on the subject of outside sources, now would probably be a good time to discuss the vast amount of genealogical material to be found in this country's official records of its populace. Because later chapters of the book address these official sources individually, this chapter will mention only the various methods of documentation used for the material found in the governmental agencies.

There are four principal methods of recording the data sources and each one has its own particular advantage for your ancestral problem-solving. The first and most valid is by directly copying the original record. A problem with this is that these records are sometimes difficult to obtain and usually fragile and irreplaceable. An acceptable way of handling those that you have, would be to photocopy the original and file away the precious record for safekeeping. The copy can then be used safely for record system.

At times, the original source material is found only in a public place and the information must be hand-recorded. It would then be expedient to *abstract* the data; that is, make a written summary of the important material. You can do this with an outline or in a narrative form, making sure to include all of the necessary information.

A quicker, if not as thorough a method of recording source material, is by *extracting* the data from the document. This consists of noting only that information required for your research problems. When copying a deed, for example, you would list only the date, the principals, and the property location; or in listing a will, by noting the date, the testator, the heirs, and the legacies.

The last method of data documentation and the most comprehensive, is by *excerpting* or, as some call it, *transcribing* the material. Occasionally all of the information from a source is needed. You will need to make an exact copy of the record, by hand, if necessary, complete with any unusual spelling or grammar. This type of recording has the benefit of imparting the data accurately while retaining the quaint flavor of the original document. One thing to remember though, in transcribing your notes. If you do encounter a strange or unfamiliar word or phrase, don't forget to add the word *(sic)* which means, "just so," and indicates that a quoted passage that may contain errors is precisely reproduced.

While we are discussing accurate and comprehensive data recording, there is one area that in the past has given rise to much confusion in regard to the dating of events for particular forebears. This confusion is especially evident if the ancestral dates happen to fall between the years 1582 and 1752 and the dates January 1 through March 25.

From the time of the Nicene Council in A.D. 365, the calendar in use by the Christian world had been the Julian calendar, named for Julius Caesar, who first introduced it in 46 B.C. This calendar divided the year into 365 days with an extra day once every four years for a leap year, much as is done today. However, later as man became more knowledgeable, it was discovered that the Julian calendar exceeded the actual solar year by eleven minutes or twenty-four hours every 131 years.

By the year 1582, the excess time measured about ten days, an amount that threw off the date for the vernal equinox and, in turn, disturbed the calculations for Easter. Pope Gregory XIII, head of the Roman Catholic Church at the time, decreed that the ten days should be dropped from the calendar in all Catholic countries in order that the vernal equinox be restored to its proper time. This changed March 11 to March 22, the correct date for the equinox. He also decreed that in order to eliminate this discrepancy in the future, leap year's extra day should be omitted three times within every 400-year period, exclusive of century years that are leap years only if divisible by 400. This was calculated to take care of the excess time and make the new calendar right with the solar year.

The Pope's decree further directed that the new year of 1582 should start with January 1 instead of the traditional March 25. This change had the effect of creating a short year of nine months and seven days in 1581 making December 31 the last day of the year instead of March 24. Because the year 1582 started earlier by two months and twenty-four days, those born in the time period between January 1 and March 24 officially became a whole year older since birth dates are calculated by calendar years.

To complicate matters further, the English speaking countries and their colonies, not being of the Catholic faith, were not inclined to follow the directives of a Catholic leader and so declined to make this calendar change until 170 years later. In the year 1752, England and her colonies were finally directed by Parliament to change to the Gregorian calendar since by this date, the time discrepancy amounted to eleven days. It was decreed that these eleven days be dropped from the calendar by having September 2 followed by September 14. Also, by the same law, the new year of 1752 was to begin on January 1, instead of the traditional March 25, in keeping with Gregorian calendar.

In order to ascertain just what these changes mean to someone attempting to establish ancestor dates, you need to keep several things in mind. For one, only those born between the years 1582 and 1752 and the dates of January 1 and March 25 are affected. To adjust to the new style from the old style, you need to add one year and eleven days to the old date to be absolutely accurate. To simplify things, many in the American colonies in the 170-year span between calendar changes began using a system called "double dating," in which the two different years were indicated without adjusting for the eleven days as in "13 February 1632/33." If you do not desire to make any adjustment of dates, you can merely indicate, as others have done, that the date you are using is the old style or "O.S." If you do want to change the date, indicate that it is the new style or "N.S."

It has been said that George Washington changed his actual old style birthdate of 11 February 1731 to the new style of 22 February 1732 to conform with the Gregorian calendar when it became official in the colonies in 1752. Had he not made this change, future generations in America would celebrate the birthdates of its two most illustrious presidents, Abraham Lincoln and George Washington, on the two consecutive dates of February 11 and 12, a most unusual occurrence.

CHAPTER 4

Cemeteries: Adventures in Graveyards

> I never realized that there was history, close at hand, beside my very own home. I did not realize that the old grave among the brambles that stood at the foot of our farm was history.
>
> —Stephan Leacock

One of the most intriguing and captivating areas of interest an ancestor hunter can investigate is that of tombstones in old cemeteries. There are many of these old, neglected, and forgotten graveyards, known only to a few nearby residents, or to someone who may have a long-dead ancestor still interred there. Sometimes the remains of an old family graveyard can still be seen on the outskirts of a farming area, containing long-gone relatives of the original land owners whose descendants may still own the land. Unfortunately, few records were kept in earlier days of these private family burial places since there were no official agencies concerned with death certificates and burial arrangements as there are today.

Town cemeteries, especially those near large cities, are much more organized, particularly with their more recent records. This is mainly due to legislation requiring that this information be made available to the public. There are private cemeteries, usually corporate-owned and run like a business resulting in quite extensive burial records. There are also church cemeteries that contain mostly members of that church. If the church is no longer there, it may be difficult to find the cemetery records since the sexton of the church usually maintained them. But, on occasion, they have been transferred to the town clerk if the sexton is no longer available.

Old tombstones can be a source of much value to the ancestor researcher. Sometimes, such information as a birth date, death date, names of children, names of parents, name of spouse, and more regarding the deceased can be found on the marker. Visiting one of these early graveyards where an ancestor might be buried is not always the easiest thing to do, especially if you no longer live near the locale where your earlier ancestors lived and died. This is where an out-of-town relative would come in handy, assuming, of course, that there is one convenient to the area of your interest.

If, for example, any of your ancestors are buried in a cemetery near where a relative of yours resides, it could be very rewarding for you if he or she would be kind enough to visit the cemetery and photograph all of the graves that bear the surnames of the ancestors being researched and send the pictures to you. This genealogical material can be very valuable to your research and most relatives are usually very accommodating as, after all, it's their family too. They are usually happy to contribute, especially if you, as the family historian, promise to send them copies of the family pedigree somewhere along the way.

Of course you can do the same thing if the family burial plot happens to be in your area. Some old graveyards can be a veritable gold mine of information since family groups were frequently buried together in the same family plot. And the inscriptions on the tombstones sometimes refer to the origin of the individual or his or her relationship to others in the family.

Occasionally, however, you will find that the inscriptions are almost illegible or obliterated and nearly impossible to read. You may have to do a rubbing of the stone by placing a large piece of paper over it and rubbing the paper with a soft lead pencil until the inscription stands out. If you desire to photograph a gravestone, it would be best to first trace the inscription with a piece of white chalk until the letters stand out more legibly. Some old cemeteries have fallen into disuse and neglect and weeds may have taken over almost the entire area of the graves. Even though it may take some little effort on your part, the ability to find and decipher the inscriptions on a tombstone can be very rewarding.

Many times in reading the engravings on tombstones you will find comments of a personal nature regarding the departed one expressing the sentiments of those who were left behind. One such epitaph that seems to echo the feeling of loss that a family may experience from the death of a loved one was found on an old gravestone as follows:

GONE BEFORE US, O OUR BROTHER,
TO THE SPIRIT LAND.
VAINLY LOOK WE FOR ANOTHER,
IN THY PLACE TO STAND.

The warning on this tombstone, found in an old Ohio graveyard, can be seen echoed on many other graves; it could be described as a rather lugubrious last word to the living:

REMEMBER ME AS YOU PASS BY.
AS YOU ARE NOW, SO ONCE WAS I.
AS I AM NOT, SO YOU MUST BE.
PREPARE FOR DEATH AND FOLLOW ME.

The sorrowful epitaph on a one-year-old infant's grave reflects the sad philosophy of its grieving parents:

HAPPY INFANT, EARLY BLEST.
LOST IN PEACEFUL SLUMBER REST.
EARLY RESERVED FROM CARES,
WHICH INCREASE WITH GROWING YEARS.

An ode on the tombstone of a sixteen-year-old boy has this comment to make:

HOW SHORT THE RACE OUR FRIEND HAS RUN,
CUT OFF IN ALL HIS BLOOM.
THE COURSE BUT YESTERDAY BEGUN,
NOW FINISHED IN THE TOMB.

An epitaph on the grave of a 63-year-old man in a Butler, Ohio cemetery reads, if not entirely poetically, at least optimistically:

GO HOME DEAR FRIENDS AND SHED NO TEARS.
I MUST LAY HERE TIL CHRIST APPEARS.
AND THEN I AM IN HOPES TO HAVE,
THE JOYFUL RISING FROM THE GRAVE.

Although most of these sentiments are usually touching, expressing sorrow and loss, there are wry or humorous inscriptions to be found. Occasionally one even encounters a bit of history on a tombstone. In a graveyard just outside of Bodie, California, an abandoned gold mining town, there is a rather poignant tale engraved on the marker of the town's founder, Waterman S. Bodey, which reads:

BURIED HERE ARE THE MORTAL REMAINS OF
WATERMAN S. BODEY, 1814-1859,
NATIVE OF POUGHKEEPSIE, NEW YORK.
NEAR HERE JUNE 20,1859,
BODEY, ALONG WITH HIS PARTNER AND
BURRO, STRUCK GOLD. FOUR MONTHS LATER
RETURNING WITH SUPPLIES HE LOST HIS LIFE
IN A BLINDING SNOWSTORM. THIS SMALL STURDY
INDOMITABLE MAN LEFT BODIE TO POSTERITY
NEVER KNOWING ITS IMPORTANCE.

As a postscript to the above story, Bodie's main claim to fame today is as a ghost town, a reminder of the days when it and other towns like it were instantly created by the gold fever and just as instantly abandoned. As a tourist attraction, it is visited only by occasional passers-by on their way to more important destinations. Sic transit gloria. . . .

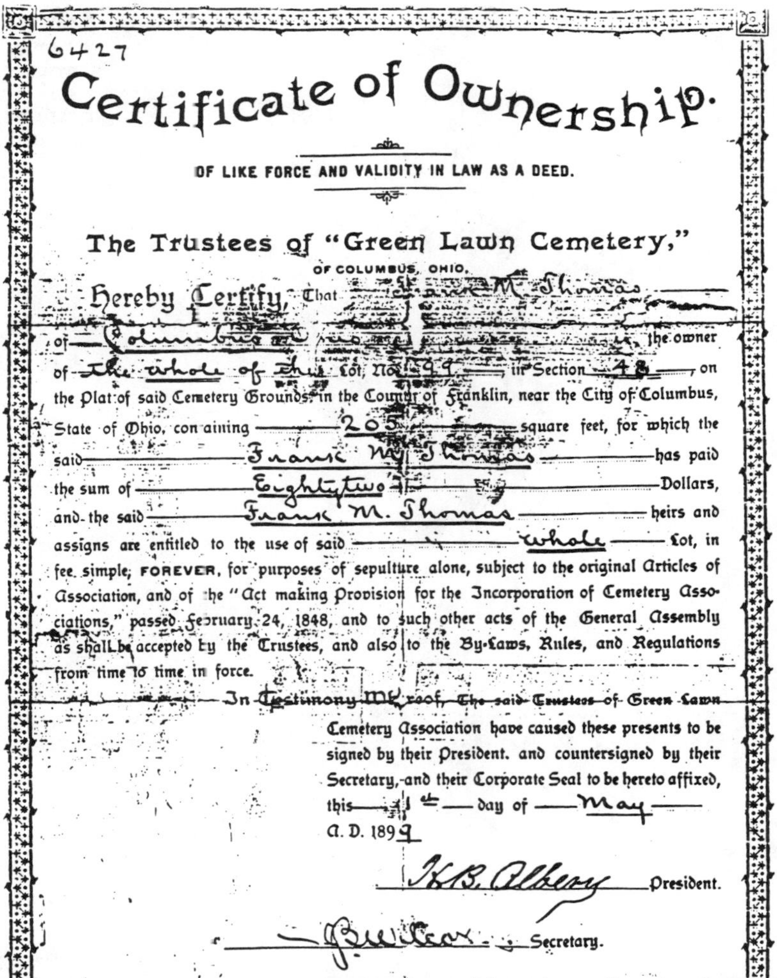

6427

Certificate of Ownership.

OF LIKE FORCE AND VALIDITY IN LAW AS A DEED.

The Trustees of "Green Lawn Cemetery,"

OF COLUMBUS, OHIO,

Hereby Certify, That Frank M. Thomas of Columbus the owner of the whole of this Lot, No. 99, in Section 48, on the Plat of said Cemetery Grounds, in the County of Franklin, near the City of Columbus, State of Ohio, containing 205 square feet, for which the said Frank M. Thomas has paid the sum of Eightytwo Dollars, and the said Frank M. Thomas heirs and assigns are entitled to the use of said whole Lot, in fee simple, FOREVER, for purposes of sepulture alone, subject to the original Articles of Association, and of the "Act making Provision for the Incorporation of Cemetery Associations," passed February 24, 1848, and to such other acts of the General Assembly as shall be accepted by the Trustees, and also to the By-Laws, Rules, and Regulations from time to time in force.

In Testimony Whereof, The said Trustees of Green Lawn Cemetery Association have caused these presents to be signed by their President, and countersigned by their Secretary, and their Corporate Seal to be hereto affixed, this 1st day of May A. D. 1899

H. B. Albery President.

[illegible] Secretary.

Figure 6a: Burial Plot Deed

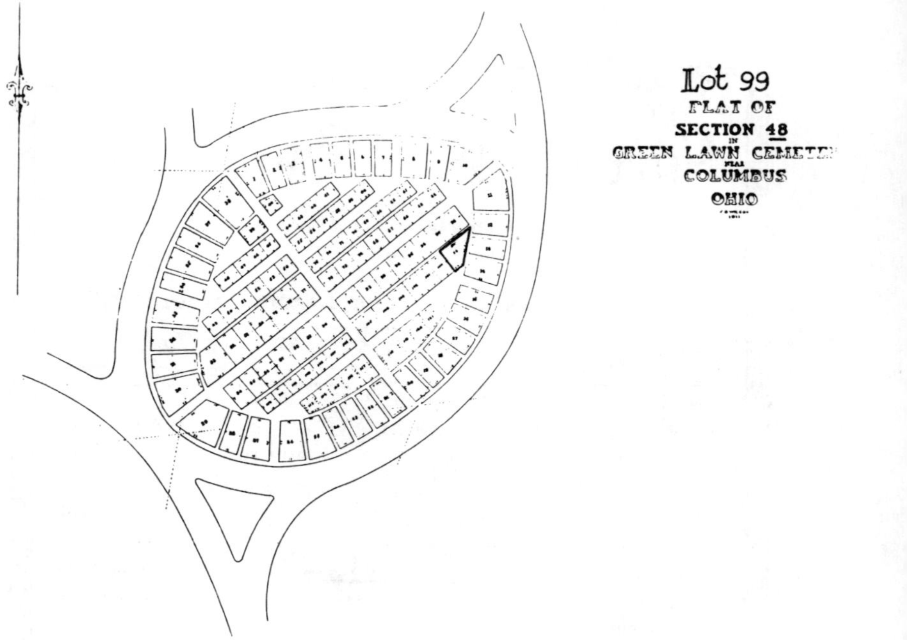

Lot 99
PLAT OF
SECTION 48
IN
GREEN LAWN CEMETE
NEAR
COLUMBUS
OHIO

SECTION 48 LOT 99

:6613	Rowland D. Thomas	(son)	(1)	May 1, 1899
:9496	Jeannette Thomas	(daughter)	(2)	Oct. 4, 1901
:6667	Margaret Thomas	(wife)	(3)	July 5, 1937
:0073	Frank M. Thomas	(Owner)	(4)	Sept. 16, 1940

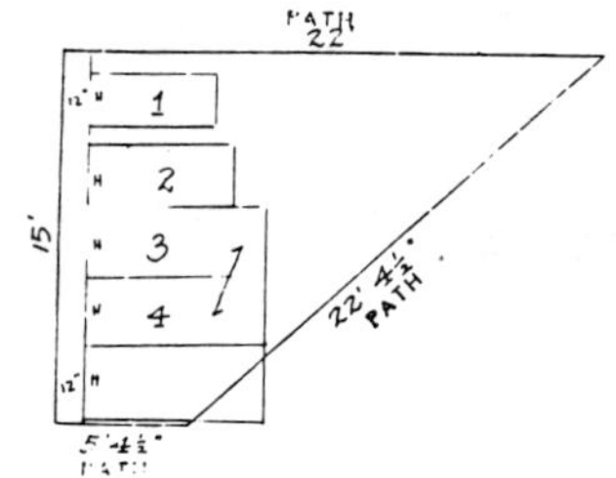

Figure 6b: Burial Plot Map

Figure 7: Tombstone

CHAPTER 5

Churches

> I never weary of great churches; it is my favorite kind of scenery. Mankind was never so happily inspired as when it made a cathedral.
>
> —Robert Louis Stevenson

America, a land whose original settlers came seeking a place free from religious intolerance or from persecution by higher authorities, remains today a country without a national church. This was not merely by chance. In the early days of colonial America there was a definite desire by some of the colonies to separate the church from the state. No doubt, they feared interference from the state into what church authorities considered to be church business only, a problem that had plagued the church in other countries in the past.

In the zeal to separate the secular from the ecclesiastical, even the act of marriage as a civil contract was declared illegal for the ministers of these churches to perform. Because of this, most mention of marriages in the records of these early churches have to do with the posting of marriage banns or the intentions to marry. Later this restriction was lifted and today, even though church and state are still separate in the United States, ministers are permitted to perform the marriage ceremony.

The desire for apartness from government was not shared by all of the colonies, however, and some did attempt to establish state churches. Evidence of these churches can still be seen in some New England states. The matter of state churches was finally decided by the drafters of the United States Constitution, who, in that document, officially separated the church from any control of state or nation. This probably seemed feasible to the founding fathers after reviewing the many different denominations that had been brought to the fledgling country by the early European settlers, all of whom naturally pressed for the installation of their religion as the official national one.

The early policy of separation of the church from the state brought about a proliferation of religions in the United States resulting in a vast number of different houses of worship of various denominations. This particular fact, along with a few others, can make researching church records a difficult task for the intrepid ancestor hunter, especially if the ancestor's religious affiliation is not known.

The first problem with researching church records is how to locate them. You must first know the denomination of the ancestor being researched in order to look into the records. If you do not know, a little investigation is needed first in order to simplify your search later. You could check, for example, old family papers such as wills and birth and death records which might give a clue to the ancestor's religious preference. An old obituary might tell or even an inscription on his tombstone might mention his religion.

If you are unable to determine the denomination, you might have to research all of the churches in your area of interest to locate this information. If you can locate a church near where your ancestor resided, write to its present minister asking for any information he might have regarding your ancestor telling when he lived in the area and when he died, if known. It might be best to send letters to all of the churches in the area even if you think you know your ancestor's religious preference; people have been known to switch churches even as they do now, and you may find records in more than one church. If the local minister does not have the old records, he might know where they can be obtained.

Occasionally, old records of churches have been collected and sent to the state organization of the church or to the state's historical society. Genealogical libraries also have some publications that document the records of certain churches—usually listed under a particular locale—which might require a little digging on your part.

Even if you are able to locate the church records, you should keep one very important thought in mind. Church records, especially the early ones, were intended to present the record of a church and its membership to the higher church authorities. Therefore, the records were considered the property of the church, and the information in them, the church's private affair. The documentation was usually done by the minister and the records retained by either him or a clerk. They were not kept in any particular order, sometimes being entered quite some time after an event took place. Occasionally, the family's records were not even documented until the parents became members of the church at a later date.

Although finding the church records might be time-consuming and exasperating at times, the information found in them can be quite rewarding. For example, you may find records of baptisms, burials, and marriage banns. Other types of church records include confirmations, membership lists, and removal and arrival records. These last two, in particular, can indicate the movements of individuals from area to area. The records also can present cases of church members who had fallen from grace and were subject to church discipline for such infractions as intoxication, profanity, and any other type of behavior the church considered improper.

For other sources of information regarding church records, there is an excellent book by E. Kay Kirkham, entitled *A Survey of American Church Records,* published by Everton Publishers, Logan, Utah. It lists many of the major denominations in existence over a century ago, especially in those states east of the Mississippi.

Another huge collection of church records is located at Salt Lake City in the Genealogical Department of the Church of the Latter Day Saints. It has a vast number of microfilmed copies of church records, not only of American churches, but of those from around the world. These records are available for public review through interlibrary loan through any branch library of the Latter Day Saints Church.

The Daughters of the American Revolution also have a large collection of church and cemetery records from every state available for review in the society's extensive library in Washington, D.C.

CHAPTER 6

Genealogical Libraries

> A great library contains the diary of the human race. The great consulting room of a wise man is a library.
>
> —G. DAWSON

Some of the most interesting and informative sources of material available to the ancestor hunter can be found in the many books and journals located in genealogical libraries. The printed family histories in these libraries contain much of value for the genealogical researcher. You may discover facts regarding family members that can open new doors to your research. Besides family histories these libraries also include books of passenger lists, compiled records of military service, city directories, cemetery records, printed abstracts of wills and deeds, and christening records of certain churches, to name a few.

However, it is important to remember that the printed material found in these libraries should not always be accepted at face value even if the information seems to fit your own family situation. All of the facts that you garner regarding the lines you are investigating should be thoroughly verified by checking more official records as accurately and as carefully as you can. Frequently, printed genealogies are published by individuals using other printed material for reference that was also found in published genealogies, thus compounding any errors that might have been made in the original

SUTRO LIBRARY
A BRANCH OF THE CALIFORNIA STATE LIBRARY*
Services in Local History and Genealogy

Availability of Services
As a branch of the California State Library, Sutro Library is a free public library. There are no charges for its services.
Hours of Opening
Open to the public from 10:00 to 9:00, Monday; 10:00 to 5:00, Tuesday through Saturday; closed Sundays and state holidays.
Collections
Genealogical material for all states except California. For genealogy, history, and other records relating to California, please consult the California State Library's California Section (in Sacramento) through your local library.
FAMILY HISTORIES: Approximately 8,000. Most are available on interlibrary loan.
LOCAL (STATE, REGIONAL, COUNTY, AND TOWN): Approximately 30,000, including town, court, birth, marriage, death, cemetery, church, and land records; wills, deeds, early "vanity" books of biographical and genealogical sketches; historical and genealogical journals. Particularly strong for eastern and midwestern states, for the records of southern states and early English parishes. Most are available on interlibrary loan.
DIRECTORIES: Approximately 8,000 city directors and 10,000 telephone directors for all parts of the United States and some foreign countries. Available for use in the library.
FEDERAL CENSUS RECORDS ON MICROFILM: All existing population schedules for the years 1800 through 1900 (including soundexes). Available to California libraries for use on interlibrary loan.
INDIAN CENSUS RECORDS ON MICROFILM: Approximately 700 rolls of microfilm of the United States Bureau of Indian Affairs censuses of reservation Indians from 1885 to 1940.
DAR LINEAGE BOOKS: 166 volumes of lineages of members of the National Society of the Daughters of the American Revolution. DAR transcripts of California pioneer family, Bible, and cemetery records.
BOSTON TRANSCRIPT FILE: Two filing cabinets of newspaper clippings from the column that appeared from 1906 to 1941, arranged in surname order.
PERIODICALS: Major national genealogical publications, major historical society journals, many local historical and genealogical society and family association newsletters. San Francisco newspapers on microfilm for the latter half of the 19th century.

Figure 8: Sutro Library Services
Sutro Library, San Francisco, California
(Reprinted courtesy of the Genealogical Association of Sacramento)

SAN FRANCISCO PUBLIC LIBRARY GENEALOGY COLLECTION: Approximately 6,000 volumes, formerly in SFPL. Available for use in the Sutro Library. Special indexes, guides, bibliographies, and additional support material to aid in genealogical and historical research.

HOW TO USE THE LIBRARY

Sutro Library works through established interlibrary loan channels to supplement services of local public libraries. Thus, request, whether for specific books or for subject information, should be initiated through a patron's local public library. Brief searches are made on subject request by the Sutro Library staff, but we ask patrons to undertake an extensive research in the Library themselves.

List of Holdings

Sutro Library maintains an extensive and detailed card catalog and subject index to its collections. Copies of the Sutro Library Genealogical Card Catalog on 48x negative microfiche can be purchased from Commercial Microfilm Service, 14200 NE 21st, Bellevue, Washington 98007. This microfiche edition of Sutro Library's Genealogical Card Catalog contains: (1) An alphabetic listing under surname of family histories that have been indexed by the library staff; and (2) a local history catalog arranged alphabetically by state and county with general histories and records for a state or county appearing first, followed by local histories and records arranged alphabetically under cities, counties, and parishes.

Photoduplication Services

Two coin-operated copying machines are available in Sutro Library for use by patrons. It is suggested that patrons bring rolls of coins for photocopying purposes. If a large quantity of reproduction is to be done, arrangements can be made with the Library for xeroxing. Microfilms, photostats, and photographs can be ordered as well. To place an order, written authorization and instructions are needed with the name and address of the person to be billed.

Sutro Library
480 Winston Drive
(San Francisco State University campus)
San Francisco, California

publication. This does not mean that all of the material you find in a printed family history is incorrect; it means merely that one should use caution in using only these documented histories in your research without proper verification with other, more official sources.

There are many large and important genealogical collections as well as many small good ones. Many public libraries have a genealogical section that sometimes can hold a surprising amount of information for the genealogical researcher. Many state libraries also have collections of some printed family histories as well as microfilm of other genealogical material. Sometimes the older sources can be found in the state archives.

The Genealogical Society of the Church of Jesus Christ of Latter Day Saints, also known as the Mormon Church, and located in Salt Lake City, Utah, has probably the largest collection of genealogical material in the world. The LDS church started its genealogical organization in 1894 to assist its own members in tracing their ancestors. The society has data consisting not only of myriad books on family histories, but has also microfilmed material of such things as church, cemetery, and marriage records, deeds, and land grants. It has also microfilmed copies of all the census and military records that have been microfilmed by the federal government. All of this material is available for public review.

Many of these microfilmed records are available through interlibrary loan for a small fee. If there is a branch library of the Latter Day Saints near you, contact it to find out the procedures necessary to obtain this material. Each branch of the LDS church also has its own considerable collection of genealogical information that can be reviewed at that particular location.

The National Society of the Daughters of the American Revolution, located in Memorial Continental Hall in Washington, D.C., has a library that contains much of genealogical value, such as military, pension, and bounty land records as well as family Bibles and tombstone inscriptions. It also contains some mortality schedules from the 1850 through 1880 censuses.

The Daughters of the American Revolution have a particular interest in the military records of the Revolutionary War since membership in this society is based upon an individual's descent from an ancestor who served as a member of the American Continental Army during that war.

The New England Historic Genealogical Society's library in Boston, Massachusetts, was founded in 1845 and today has probably the world's largest genealogical book library in the world with a collection of volumes covering all of the states and some foreign countries. It also publishes a periodical devoted to genealogy, the *New England Historical and Genealogical Register,* in which the genealogies of many families from throughout the United States as well as New England, have been published.

To become a member of the Society, advertised as the oldest and largest non-profit genealogical society in America, write to: The New England Historic Genealogical Society, 101 Newbury Street, Boston, Massachusetts 02116. At present the fee is $45.00 a year for a full membership, which includes such services as a quarterly journal and bimonthly magazine, a book loan service, and a genealogical research service available for an hourly fee. Write directly to the Society for further information on other services available to members and their families.

The Library of Congress, the official library of the United States, located on Capitol Hill in Washington, D.C., has a huge collection of genealogies, not only of American families but of those in many foreign countries. One of its publications, a two-volume book called *Genealogies in the Library of Congress,* lists the variety of genealogical material found in the library. A copy of this publication can usually be found in most public libraries.

There are, of course, many other large genealogical libraries usually in the larger cities such as New York, Chicago, San Francisco, and Los Angeles, to name a few. Because the books in these libraries are rare, for the most part, they are not available through inter-library loan and must be reviewed in person. However, before you spend money for such a trip, review all of your local libraries to see what you can find there; you might be surprised to find much of what you need right in your own neighborhood. Any information you obtain locally can be useful even if you do decide later to travel over a distance to a larger library.

UNRECORDED WILLS AND INVENTORIES, MONMOUTH CO., N. J. 23

". . . & bringing up of my Son John untill he shall Attaine . . . . One and Twenty yeares and . . . that "my Son liue with my said Executor untill he shall be of Age . . . and that he learne the Carpenters trade and to "Read & write if Capeable . . ."

Wits.: THERLAGH ſwijny
Peter Tilton
William Lawrence junor
Thomas Waimeright [his mark]
John ffish [his mark]
Richd Gardiner
Entered upon the Records of Pro. of East New Jersey, "this XXXIst of March, 1684," in lib. A., fol. 65, "Ja. Emott, Dep[t] Secrety."

WILL of GILBERT LANE, of Middletown, Co. of Mon., yeoman, "being in health of Body." Dated Nov. 7th, 1720. Proved by oath of John Little, wit., that he "saw the other" wits. sign; before Michael Kearny, Surr., Perth Amboy, 17th May, 1727.

Gives: "unto my Loving wife Jane Lane all my Goods and Chattels during her life"; "unto my Sons Adrian Lane "Cornelius Lane and Matthias Lane, and my Daughters Moika Longstreet Catharine Dehart Mary Van Sicklah[n?] Jane "Lane and my Grand children which were born of my Daughter Williamca Hendrickson late Deceased, formerly wife of "William Hendrickson likewise Deceased after my wifes decease all my Personal Estate . . . to be Equally divided "between them . . . in Eight Equal parts . . . And as Concerning my Son Joseph Lane who is blind, My will ". . . is That within Six weeks after my own and my wifes decease and before my Estate is Parted . . . among "my Seven first Mentioned children and the Children of my Daughter Williamca Hendrickson that all my . . . Seven "children and my Aforesd Grandchildren shall Give bond of two Hundred pounds unto Each other with Conditions that "Each . . . shall bear their Equall part . . . according to the Discretion of my Executors in the Keeping and "Maintaining their Said Brother Joseph Lane yearly . . . During his natural life. But if any of my Said Children ". . . Refuse to Give Bond . . . they Shall lose their Equal parts . . . of my Estate and be Entirely out "of from Enjoying any part of my Estate and their parts that shall so refuse to be Equally divided among thos that "shall Perform my will . . ."

Appoints "my Sd Sons Adrian, Cornelius and Mathias Lane Executors . . ."

Wits.: GILBERT LANE [his mark]
John Little
Saml Dennis
Jacob Dennis

Oath of Executors, Adrian, Cornelius and Mathias Lane, before Michael Kearny, Surro., appointed by William Burnet, Esq[r], Gov. in Chief, Perth Amboy, May 17, 1727.
Recorded in Lib. B., fol. 66 & 67, Mich. Kearny, D. Reg[r].

INVENTORY of EDMOND SMITH, of Midletowne, Late deceased, by Eliſha Lawrance and Richard Stout. Dated May 6, 1704. Proved by oath of Eliſha Lawrance and Richard Stout, before Obadiah Bowne, Juſtice, May 19th, [No year], and also by oath of Elisha Lawrence, "one of the appraisers," before Thomas Reuell, Esq., Surrogate, Middletowne, May 22, 1704.

Items of Interest:	£ s d
"his wearing apprel	0—13—00
"his tooles	0—03—00
"Cattle	— — —
	Total about £29—00—00
"allso may 19th then apprised by us "tweluе ſheep	£ 3—05—00

"Eliſha Lawrence
"Richard Stout"

Figure 9: Unrecorded Wills and Inventories
Monmouth County, New Jersey

CHAPTER 7

Vital Statistics

> History is a pact between the dead, the living, and the yet unborn.
>
> —EDMUND BURKE

Vital statistics are official records that concern themselves with probably the three most important happenings in an individual's life: his birth, his marriage, and his death. Those vital records concerned with the beginning and the end of one's existence contribute some of the most important data to be found in regard to the individual and his personal statistics.

At first, the use of vital statistics in the United States was confined to the individual states with New England the most prominent in keeping such records. Not until 1879, when the National Board of Health was created by Congress, was there an emphasis placed upon the states to use a standardized death certificate. The establishment of a federal health department was probably due, in part, to the growing concern regarding the necessity to keep track of the deaths of victims of plagues and epidemics. The government believed that these statistics were indeed vital in order to attempt to control any further outbreaks of cholera or any of the other prevalent diseases taking their toll of lives at that time. Government intervention and direction seemed to be the only answer to controlling these outbreaks.

Although many states did begin to officially record births and deaths around 1850, such records were not generally kept until after 1890, when the federal government suggested that the states use a standardized form for their birth and death records. Most of the states did, although some were slower than others to use the recommended standard form for their official vital records. Today, every state has its own particular office that handles vital statistics; sometimes it can be found in the department of vital statistics and other times in the health department. Occasionally, the records can be found in the county of occurrence instead of the state; a check with the state would reveal this.

Vital records can contain much important data concerning an individual. For example, death certificates, at least in later years, can list the father, the mother, their places of birth, the father's occupation, and the mother's maiden name, and sometimes the funeral home that handled the burial. However, the information given on death certificates is only as accurate as the person giving it. This is usually the next of kin, who, through lack of knowledge or emotional upset, might pass on the wrong information. Don't be too upset if the information doesn't exactly correlate with your own. Mistakes do happen when dealing with the human variable.

Birth records are a trifle more difficult to obtain than death records, because the event occurred so much earlier in time. If the county or state office does not have a birth record, then the next best place to look might be the family Bible, or failing that, a church record. Unfortunately, church records usually give christening dates only, but at least the date is close to that of the birth. These records also list the father and mother of the infant.

Marriage records in some areas, especially the original thirteen states, go quite far back. The information usually gives the names of the bride and groom and where they are from. If the records cannot be located in the offices of the state or county, then try the records of old churches for marriage banns or intentions to marry. The banns preceded the marriage, of course, and if banns are found, one can usually assume a marriage took place, but not always. Occasionally, even in that day, human nature being what it is, the betrothed couple wound up married to other people. So be forewarned; even those records can sometimes be erroneous.

One very valuable book, *The Handy Book for Genealogists,*

Everton Publishers, Inc., found in most genealogical libraries, tells of the availability and location of birth, death, and marriage records in all of the states and their counties and in some foreign countries. This book lists documented sources of where these and other records can be found. In contacting these sources for information, it is advisable to send all of the information you know of the ancestor being researched. If an exact date of the event being checked is unknown, give the approximate date. Some of the individuals doing the research will take the time to canvas their records quite thoroughly. There will be a charge for sending you copies, which will vary from state to state. When requesting a search ask what the fees are for the service and you will usually receive a reply by return mail.

No SOCIAL SECURITY NO.

STATE OF ILLINOIS ORIGINAL
HENRY HORNER, GOVERNOR
Department of Public Health—Division of Vital Statistics

CERTIFICATE OF DEATH

1. PLACE OF DEATH. County of COOK, Registration Dist. No. 3104
City of CHICAGO Primary Dist. No. 3104
Street and Number, No. 1416 E 63rd Pl St., 6 Ward. Registered No. 25911 (Consecutive No.) Hospital.
(If death occurred in a hospital or institution, give its NAME instead of street and number.)
LENGTH OF TIME AT PLACE WHERE DEATH OCCURED? yrs. 6 mos. ds.

1a. PLACE OF RESIDENCE: STATE Ill. County Cook Township Road Dist.
(Usual place of abode) City Chicago Street and Number 1416 E 63rd Pl

2. FULL NAME Frank M. Thomas 83 A

PERSONAL AND STATISTICAL PARTICULARS

3. SEX Male
4. COLOR OR RACE White
5. Single, Married, Widowed, or Divorced (write the word) Widower
5a. If married, widowed, or divorced HUSBAND of (or) WIFE of Margaret Thomas
6. DATE OF BIRTH (month, day, and year) Aug 28 - 1855
7. AGE Years 85 Months 0 Days 13 IF LESS than 1 day, hrs. or min.

OCCUPATION
8. Trade, profession, or particular kind of work done, as spinner, sawyer, bookkeeper, etc. Fireman
9. Industry or business in which work was done, as silk mill, saw mill, bank, etc. Columbus Fire Dept
10. Date deceased last worked at this occupation (month and year) June 1925
11. Total time (years) spent in this occupation 30

12. BIRTHPLACE (city or town) West Jefferson (State or country) Ohio

FATHER
13. NAME James Thomas
14. BIRTHPLACE (city or town) unknown (State or country) Wales

MOTHER
15. MAIDEN NAME Delia Titus
16. BIRTHPLACE (city or town) unknown (State or country) New York City

17. INFORMANT Jeannette Lane (personal signature with pen and ink)
P. O. Address 1416 E 63rd Pl

18. PLACE OF BURIAL, Cremation or Removal
Cemetery Greenlawn
19. DATE 9-14 1940
Location Columbus (Township, Road Dist., Village or City)
County State Ohio

20. UNDERTAKER Thos E Corcoran (personal signature with pen and ink) (firm name, if any)
ADDRESS 1411 E 67 St

Has decedent ever served in military or naval service of U. S.? No

MEDICAL CERTIFICATE OF DEATH

21. DATE OF DEATH (month, day, and year) 9/12 1940
22. I HEREBY CERTIFY, That I attended deceased from 1-1-40, 193 to 9/12/1940
I last saw him alive on 9/12/1940, death is said to have occurred on the date stated above, at 6:20 p. m.
*The principal cause of death and related causes of importance were as follows: Date of onset

Cerebral Hemorrhage 9/11/40

Other contributory causes of importance:
Arteriosclerosis 1-1-36
Ch. bronchitis 4-1-40

23. Was an operation performed? no Date of —
For what disease or injury? —
Was there an autopsy? no
What test confirmed diagnosis? clinical
24. If a communicable disease; where contracted? —
Was disease in any way related to occupation of deceased? no
If so, specify how:
(Signed) H Hugh Cox M. D.
Address 2376 E 71st St
Date 9/12 1940 Telephone Dor 0311

*N. B.—State the disease causing death. All cases of death from "violence, casualty, or any undue means" must be referred to the coroner. See Section 10 Coroner's Act.

25. Filed 193 Herman N. Bundesen Registrar.
P. O. Address 1940 SEP 13 PM 8 53

Figure 10: Certificate of Death

STATE OF MAINE

COPY OF A RECORD OF LIVE BIRTH

OFFICE OF THE CLERK OF Norridgewock, MAINE

CHILD	FULL NAME OF CHILD: Edith Hazel Collins			
	BIRTHPLACE: Norridgewock, Maine			
	DATE OF BIRTH: July 11, 1889		SEX: Female	
FATHER OF CHILD	FATHER'S NAME: Gardner Jacob Collins			
	COLOR OR RACE: white	AGE: 27	RESIDENCE: Norridgewock, Maine	
	BIRTHPLACE: New Sharon, Maine		OCCUPATION: Machinist and Farmer	
MOTHER OF CHILD	MOTHER'S MAIDEN NAME: Charlotte Ann Tibbetts			
	COLOR OR RACE: white	AGE: 19	RESIDENCE: Norridgewock, Maine	
	BIRTHPLACE: Norridgewock, Maine			
ATTENDANT AND REGISTRAR	NAME, TITLE, AND ADDRESS OF PERSON REPORTING BIRTH: Milford Tibbetts, uncle Norridgewock, Maine			
	NAME OF CLERK RECORDING THIS BIRTH: Elsie D. Stanley		DATE CERTIFICATE RECEIVED FOR FILING: February 19, 1945	

The above is a true copy of facts entered on the record of the birth of the person named hereon which is in my official custody.

ATTEST: Elaine B. Libby

CLERK OF Norridgewock, MAINE DATE ISSUED March 21, 1966

Figure 11: Record of Live Birth

MARRIAGE LICENSE.

STATE OF MISSOURI, County of Phelps

THIS LICENSE authorizes any Judge, Justice of the Peace, licensed or ordained Preacher of the Gospel, or any other person authorized under the laws of this State, to solemnize Marriage between Joseph R. Clark of Edgar Springs, County of Phelps and State of Missouri who is over the age of twenty-one years; and Armenda Mobley of Edgar Springs County of Phelps and State of Missouri who is over the age of eighteen years.

L S

WITNESS my hand as Circuit Clerk and Ex-Officio Recorder, with the seal of office hereto affixed, at my office in Rolla, Mo the 14 day of Dec, 1893

David E. Carnan
Circuit Clerk and Ex-Officio Recorder.

By H B Perry D
Deputy.

STATE OF MISSOURI,
COUNTY OF Phelps } ss.

THIS IS TO CERTIFY that the undersigned, a minister of the Gospell did, at the brides Residence in said County, on the 17' day of December, A. D. 1893, unite in marriage the above named persons.

Recorded ________ 18__

Eld Jas. A. Patterson M. G.

Figure 12: Marriage License

Chapter 8

Probate Court Records

> If rich men would remember that shrouds have no pockets, they would while living, share their wealth with their children.
>
> —Tryon Edwards

Probate court records, those records that pertain to one's estate after death, can be of great value to the ancestor hunter and the most useful of all these records is the will. Although wills are found mainly in the probate court of jurisdiction, information about wills can also be obtained from printed abstracts found in genealogical libraries and from the records of a historical society.

Wills mention many things. For example, the testator names his heirs, usually mentioning their relationship to him. His assets are listed as well as the date of his death, his residence at the time of death, and sometimes, the names of all the members of his family. Wills can also, at times, reveal personal comments, sometimes not very flattering, as to the testator's opinion of some of the heirs and relatives. It would appear to be the testator's way of getting the proverbial last word as the saying goes. Another significant statement in a will that would seem to indicate an opinion of the testator is one to the effect that a particular individual ". . . is left the sum of one dollar." This statement is necessary, one supposes, to prevent the aforementioned cut-off heir from contesting the will on the basis that the testator merely "forgot" to mention him as an heir.

There are two different kinds of wills: a written, or holographic will, and an oral, or nuncupative will. The written will is the most common used today. The nuncupative will is usually used only when one is unexpectedly dying such as happens on a battlefield and it concerns only personal property. It requires a certain amount of witnesses to make it valid. These oral wills were more common in the early days of the country since many individuals could neither read nor write. Instead they recited their wills to witnesses.

The will that an ancestor hunter would be interested in is, of course, the written one. For a thorough investigation of wills, research should probably be done in person, by you or an agent or relative. Wills need to be reviewed very carefully as a chance word may indicate something to you or an agent that a clerk might not comprehend. However, if you cannot visit a probate court in person, there are ways of obtaining copies of wills if certain facts are known about the testator and heirs.

When a will is recorded it is usually registered and indexed by the testator's name, and sometimes cross-indexed by beneficiaries' names. If you know the probate court location of an area where the ancestor died, contact the court clerk and request information on any wills under your ancestor's name. If a will is found, arrangements might be made, for a fee, to have a copy sent to you. *The Handy Book for Genealogists,* Everton Publishers, Inc., lists the locations of probate courts in all states indicating which records can be found in each county. Some of the older records may have been transferred to state archives. If this is the case, you should contact the particular state to determine what records are available.

Another record of genealogical value found in a probate court is the decree of distribution, a judgment made in cases where an individual dies intestate or without leaving a will. Distribution must be made according to law with each family member receiving a certain portion. The administrator of the will has the responsibility of submitting an inventory of the assets, paying all bills, settling all accounts, and making distribution to the proper heirs. He must also submit the decree of distribution (called different things in different courts) showing the actual names of the heirs, something a will does not always do, and their relationship to the deceased. It is this list, required by law, that is the most useful for research, since the distribution shows exactly how the estate was divided. By law, no one can be omitted, so every living heir must be mentioned by name, thus furnishing much of interest to the researcher.

Also found in probate courts are guardianship papers that relate court appointments of guardians for minor children, incompetents, and elderly seniles. The purpose of such guardianship is for the managing of the rights and property of those considered incapable of handling their own affairs. A minor child, especially in the past, could be assigned a guardian even if one or both parents were alive, particularly if a legacy were involved. The assumption was, and still is, that the minor child's assets would need the special handling that a guardianship would afford.

Guardianship papers usually include the name of the parents, the name of the child, the name of the guardian, and the relationship of guardian to ward, if any. Occasionally a child of fourteen or more could select his own guardian, subject to court approval. This sometimes occurred after the marriage of the minor's widowed mother to a second husband, or a widower father to a new wife. In some states, the natural parents can petition to become their child's guardian. In other states this is illegal and an outside guardian must be appointed. Sometimes a guardian is named by a parent in his will and this is usually the last word on the subject with the court deferring to the testator's established preference. This type of guardian is called a "testamentary guardian." A guardianship terminates when the ward reaches legal age and is able to take charge of his own affairs.

CHAPTER 9

Land Records

> The farther we get away from the land, the greater our insecurity.
>
> —HENRY FORD

The dream of land ownership was just as important a concept to the early pioneers who settled in this country's original thirteen colonies as it is to people today. Because of this, land records date back to early colonial America, furnishing such information as the property owner's name, location of the land, and its assessed value. Land was cheap and easy to obtain then and any able-bodied man who desired to acquire some on which to settle was able to do so.

Even in the days before the United States had become a sovereign power, the American colonies had been very liberal in granting land to the first settlers. After the Revolutionary War, the United States, which had acquired vast holdings of land as a result of that war, designated part of this territory as public land. The liberal policy of land grants continued as before the war, but now the United States government was the grantor instead of the individual colony.

In 1785, the Northwest Ordinance was passed offering much of this land to the general public at extremely low cost. The intent of this ordinance was to encourage the rapid settlement of the newly acquired territory in order to form new states. Also, this act first introduced the system, still in effect today, by which land is surveyed, by baselines and meridians rather than by the old, more informal metes and bounds.

The United States also offered land in public domain to veterans of certain wars as a bonus for their past military service. Called bounty land warrants, these grants were first offered in 1812 when Congress designated land in certain states for this purpose. Later, bounty land grants were offered to veterans of all wars fought through 1855, and, for the first time, could be assigned to someone else.

Before the Civil War, the federal government gave land to anyone who settled in the states of Florida, Oregon, and Washington thus allowing the United States to confirm its claim to this territory. These grants were called "donation entries," because they were given entirely free to the settlers. The United States also honored private land claims that arose when the government obtained property from another country. The acquisition of California from Mexico after the Mexican War is one such example. The settlers, who had earlier received land grants from the Mexican government, were awarded the land from the United States if the claims were proved valid. Most other private land claims were also based upon land granted to earlier settlers by foreign governments before the United States had established legal claim. These, too, were granted if the claim could be verified.

One of the most important of the later land acts passed by the United States was the Homestead Act of 1862. Under this act, U.S. citizens could apply for up to 160 acres of land in public domain. It was theirs if certain conditions were met, including living upon and improving the land for a five-year period.

Over the years, the United States has donated land in the public domain to various individuals for specific reasons. Not until 1935, did the government finally close all public land to the private sector.

The publication, *Genealogical Research in the National Archives,* can help in researching an ancestor who may have been a participant in one of these early land transactions involving the federal government. Two chapters are devoted to land grant records and bounty land warrants and are quite detailed as to the location and availability of the records in the National Archives in Washington, D.C.

Although these records are mostly from the period 1800-1973, some date back as far as 1685. Most of the records show only the name and place of residence of an applicant for purchase or grant, but in the case of private land claims, much more can be found of genealogical value, mainly because the applicant was required to show descent from an ancestor who had been the original grantee.

Researching the old land grants can be an entertaining and frequently rewarding pursuit for the intrepid ancestor hunter. But the land records of transactions between private parties is probably a more significant source of genealogical material. These land records, known as deeds, spell out the principals to the contract, the grantor (seller), and the grantee (buyer). The document also records the consideration (price) paid, the property location, the date of the contract, residences of the principals, and the witnesses to the deed.

Although land records do not reveal specific information regarding the personal statistics of an individual, such as a birthdate, they can help in other areas of genealogical interest. A deed can establish, for example, an ancestor's presence in a particular location at a specific time in history. The name of the spouse and, occasionally, the names of other members of the family may be included. Sometimes deeds can also indicate relationships between the buyer and seller, such as a transaction between children and parents. Even the economic situation of an individual can sometimes be determined by noting how much land he bought and sold.

Old deeds occasionally have rather quaint and picturesque wording, quaint by our modern standards, that is. A land description in an old deed could read: ". . . beginning at Locust Tree South of County Road about 12 inches in diameter, then a Southeast course to a Black Oak tree about 8 inches in diameter in the fork of a hollow . . ." A thought could cross one's mind, "What happens in future transactions if someone cuts down the Black Oak tree?" Perhaps this is what motivated the U.S. government to change its land surveying system to the present rectangular survey method using meridians and baselines as units of measurement instead of metes and bounds.

Some deeds can be found in probate courts, but most are located in the offices of county recorders or county clerks. Old

THIS INDENTURE, made on this Seventh day of November, A.D. One Thousand Nine Hundred and Thirty-Two by and between Sarah E. Wilson, formerly Sarah E. Underwood, widow of Pleasant M. Underwood, deceased, and J. W. Wilson, her husband, of Pulaski County, Missouri; S. F. Underwood and Frances R. Underwood, his wife, of Pulaski County, Missouri; W. S. Underwood and Alpha Underwood, his wife, of St. Louis, Missouri; D. E. Underwood and Sallie Underwood, his wife, of Ontario, California; Cathie Nichols and O. B. Nichols, her husband of the county of Cook State of Illinois Parties of the First Part, and W. E. Underwood and Edith H. Underwood, husband and wife of the county of Jefferson and State of Kansas, Parties of the Second Part.

WITNESSETH, That the said Parties of the First Part in consideration of the sum of Five Hundred ---------- Dollars to them paid by the said Parties of the Second Part, the receipt of which is hereby acknowledged, do___ by these Presents, Grant, Bargain and Sell, Convey and Confirm, unto the said Parties of the Second Part their heirs and assigns, the following described lots, Tracts or Parcels of land lying, being and situated in the county of Pulaski and State of Missouri, to-wit:

All of Lots Four (4) and Five (5) of the Northeast quarter of Section Five (5), Township Thirty-four (34), of Range Ten (10), West of the Fifth Principal Meridian, except all North and West of the County road in the Northwest corner of said Lot 5, then beginning at Locust Tree South of County road about 12 inches in diameter, then a Southeast course to a Black Oak tree about 8 inches in diameter in the fork of a hollow, then West to the boundary line, the exception containing Seven acres more or less and being in the Northwest corner of the West half of Lot 5, Section 5, Township 34 of Range 10, and the tract herein conveyed containing 153 acres more or less. The above exception is the same as excepted in a certain Deed dated December 22, 1915 of record in Book 81 at page 146 in the Recorder's office of said County, and made by John Giddens and wife to Pleasant M. Underwood.

Grantor, Sarah E. Wilson is the widow of Pleasant M.Underwood, deceased, and conveys all her interest as such widow, Grantors, S. F. Underwood, W. S. Underwood, D. E. Underwood and Cathie Nichols are sons and daughter of Pleasant M.Underwood, deceased, and each convey and undivided One - seventh interest in and to said lands, subject to the interest of Sarah E. Wilson, which is also conveyed herein by her.

Grantee, W. E. Underwood is a son and heir at law of Pleasant M. Underwood, deceased and has by inheritance an undivided One-Seventh interest in said land in addition to his rights acquired by this Deed.

U S E.W.et S
12-29-32
I .50¢ R

TO HAVE AND TO HOLD the premises aforesaid; with all and singular the Rights, Privileges, Appurtenances and Immunities thereto belonging or in anywise appertaining, unto the said Parties of the Second Part, and unto their heirs and assigns FOREVER: the said Grantors hereby Covenanting that they are lawfully seized of an Indefeasible Estate in fee; in the premises hereby conveyed; that they have good right to convey the same; that the said premises are free and clear of any incumbrances done or suffered by them or those under whom they claim; and that they will WARRANT AND DEFEND the title to said premises unto the said Parties of the Second Part, and unto their heirs and assigns FOREVER, against the lawful claims and demands of all persons whomsoever, subject to taxes on said lands, and that the interests herein conveyed are undivided as above described.

IN WITNESS WHEREOF, the said parties of the First Part have hereunto set their hands and seals the day and year first above written.

D. E. Underwood	(SEAL)	Sarah E. Wilson	(SEAL)
Sallie Underwood	(SEAL)	J. W. Wilson	(SEAL)
W. S. Underwood	(SEAL)	S. F. Underwood	(SEAL)
Alpha Underwood	(SEAL)	Frances R. Underwood	(SEAL)

Figure 13: Old Deed

deeds are sometimes in the custody of the town clerk's office. Genealogical libraries also have books of compiled lists of deeds from various areas.

To find an office of land jurisdiction, consult *The Handy Book for Genealogists,* which lists for each state the particular county office that retains copies of deeds recorded in that county. There is usually an index in the office in which you might find a name, date, and where the deed was recorded. Of course, some deeds may have been recorded later, or not at all, so even if you cannot locate a deed, this does not mean that your ancestor did not own land. A check with the state archives might reveal an old unrecorded deed that could offer a genealogical bonanza to the dedicated researcher.

Property tax records also might furnish information regarding an early ancestor. These documents show the taxes paid by a property owner to the county or city having jurisdiction over the property. These taxes are usually charged on both real and personal property. Tax records can be found in the tax collector's office or the assessor's office of the county.

Land ownership maps, old county maps published before 1900, show the names of the actual land owners at the time the maps were printed. Copies of these maps can be found in some genealogical libraries and historical societies. The Library of Congress has an extensive collection of such maps. To obtain information about its map holdings, write to the Library of Congress, the Superintendent of Documents, U.S. Printing Office, Washington, D.C. 20402, and ask for its pamphlet listing the land ownership maps and the procedures necessary to obtain copies of them.

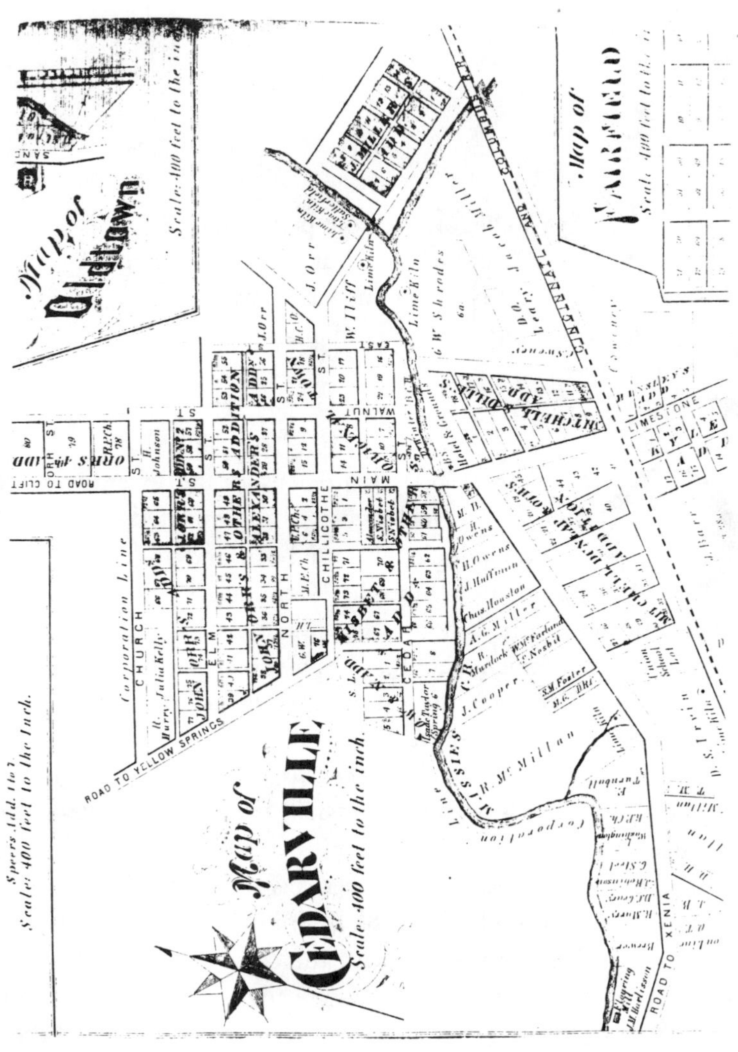

Figure 14: Land Ownership Map

CHAPTER 10

The Federal Census Records

> History can be formed from permanent monuments and records, but lives can only be written from personal knowledge which is growing every day less, and in a short time is lost forever.
>
> —Samuel Johnson

One of the most comprehensive and extensive collections of personal data ever accumulated concerning a nation's population can be found in this country's National Archives in Washington, D.C., and in its eleven branches throughout the United States. This huge and impressive government building has a vast depository of valuable information relating to the various dealings of the United States with its residents and citizens.

These documents include census, military, pension, and bounty land records as well as passenger lists and naturalization records.

Although the National Archives was not established until the 1930s, its records go back to the beginning of the Federal period in the United States starting with the country's establishment in 1776. Very few of its records predate the Revolutionary War, so not much from the colonial period can be found there. Records pertaining to this early period in the nation should be researched through historical societies and archives of the particular state.

Among the various types of records in the National Archives, the most valuable to an ancestor hunter can be the federal population schedules, known as the census records. This is especially true if your family lived in the United States prior to 1920, the last census currently available for public viewing. Because of the sensitive nature of these records, and in order to protect the privacy of individuals, census records are restricted from public review for 72 years after the census is taken.

The federal census was first taken in 1790 and has been conducted every ten years since. The 1790 and 1800 censuses were population counts taken in order to apportion representatives according to the number of people living within the states. Many people suspected they were also taken for tax reasons and, as a result, difficulties were encountered in enumerating the population. Quite a number of individuals were naturally reluctant to hand out information about themselves that could result in higher taxation, especially after their earlier experiences with Mother England on the subject.

Another reason for anonymity seemed to stem from an old fear of divine retribution, a feeling that, according to legend, someone in the family would die within the year if information was given to the census taker. The lack of conformity in how a census was taken also added to the confusion. There were no standard forms, so the censuses were taken on all different sizes and shapes of paper. It was not until 1850 that standardized forms were introduced.

Because the federal censuses of 1790 and 1800 were population counts, they named only the free heads of the house and listed the others in the house only by sex and age group. Censuses of 1810 through 1840 also named only the heads of the house, but elaborated on types of individuals such as whether they were free or slave, handicapped, and whether a citizen or alien. By 1850, a decision was made to enumerate by name all persons in the household, indicating their age, color, occupation, sex, place of birth, and value of property owned. Various additional information was recorded with each succeeding census, a fact that has certainly been a boon to all of the genealogical researchers who have since used these census records.

All of the census records at the National Archives have been

1860 FEDERAL CENSUS of the COUNTY of ....Miami.... in the STATE OF ....Ohio....

Surname ....LANE....

District Township Town or Post Office	House Number	Family Number	Names of persons living in this family	Age	Sex	Color	Occupation	Value of Real Prop.	Value of Person. Prop.	Place of Birth
Brown	278	272	Lane, Samuel	33	M	W	Farmer	450	800	New Jersey
"	"	"	" Sarah	34	F	"	Housekeeper			Ohio
"	"	"	" Mary A.	8	F	"				Ohio
"	"	"	" Franklin L.	6	M	"				Ohio
Brown	279	273	Lane, Isaac	44	M	"	Farmer	1800	900	New Jersey
"	"	"	" Salina	34	F	"	Housekeeper			Ohio
"	"	"	" Mary A.	23	F	"	At home			Ohio
"	"	"	" William	17	M	"	Farm laborer			Ohio
Brown	289	287	Lane, Charles	51	M	"	Painter	300	200	New Jersey
"	"	"	" Elizabeth	47	F	"	Housekeeper			Ohio

Figure 15: Sample Information from 1860 Federal Census

microfilmed and are available for research with the exception of the 1890 schedule, which was almost completely destroyed by fire. These records are housed not only at the main depository in Washington, D.C., but in all eleven of the archive branches (listed in the back of this book). Many local genealogical libraries have some copies of census records on hand, or for a fee, you can send for microfilm copies from the Genealogical Society Library of the Church of Jesus Christ of Latter Day Saints at Salt Lake City. It maintains copies of all the census records and can send those ordered to your local library for review. If you want your own copy of a microfilmed census record, you can buy one outright from the National Archives in Washington, D.C. If it is convenient, you can contact the closest National Archives branch to find out the price and how to obtain the microfilm.

To effectively review a census record, you need to know not only the particular county in which your ancestor lived, but also the township or city of location. Microfilmed census records are usually designated under each state by county with each township enumerated. Large cities are usually divided into districts or wards making research more difficult as it is time-consuming to look through all of these districts if the correct one is not known.

Reviewing microfilmed census records can be tedious and sometimes unrewarding, but when a missing ancestor is located, one has the feeling somewhat akin to that of the slot machine gambler who has just hit a long awaited jackpot. Occasionally, when one is studiously scanning these old records in a quiet, library atmosphere, the silence is broken by a joyous exclamation of "Eureka!" or "There you are!" addressed to the missing forebear. When the researcher glances sheepishly around and apologizes, "Well, I've been looking for him for a long time!" most of the other researchers will smile back in sympathetic understanding, knowing full well the feeling of discovery and achievement that the moment brings.

However, a thought to keep in mind is that even if you do not locate an anxiously sought forebear, that does not mean he was not in that area at census time. People were frequently missed by census takers for various reasons. Sometimes the individual was not at home and thus not mentioned to the census taker. Perhaps no one answered the door, because they were reluctant to talk to him or possibly the census taker was careless, indifferent, or incompetent. At any rate, do not rule out any of these possibilities if you do not locate an ancestor you are convinced should be there. Maybe he was. Perhaps later research will reveal his presence there.

In regard to other available microfilmed material, the National Archives is acquiring mortality records from 1850 to 1880 that show the name, date, cause of death, and place of birth of each person who died the year preceding the census year. Although the mortality schedules are not complete, certain states are available for review. State archives also have mortality schedules as do libraries, some historical societies and the Daughters of the American Revolution, 1776 D Street, NW, Washington, D.C. 20006.

A free booklet, *Genealogical Records in the National Archives,* may be obtained by writing to the National Archives and Records Service, General Services Administration, Washington, D.C. 20408. A National Archives book, *Guide to Genealogical Research in the National Archives,* can be found in most genealogical libraries, and can also be purchased from the National Archives or any of its branches. This book offers a comprehensive overview of all the material to be found in the National Archives, and offers much useful and informative instruction on how to start your own genealogical research.

CHAPTER 11

Military Records

> The men below who batter the foe,
> The men behind the guns!
>
> —JOHN JEROME ROONEY

An important genealogical source of information are the many records of the military personnel who have served in this country's armed forces. These records are located in three areas: the National Archives in Washington, D.C.; the Washington National Record Center in Suitland, Maryland; and the National Records Center in St. Louis, Missouri. Although the National Archives is not the only source of military activities information in the United States, it has probably the most comprehensive and consolidated collection of military data in the country.

The military in the United States was created August 7, 1789, when Congress established the War Department and that September authorized the re-enlistment of men in troops thus creating a standing army. Congress also authorized the commissioning of officers at that time and in 1802 the U.S. Military Academy was established at West Point, New York. At first, the War Department was in charge of all military operations, but that ceased on April 30, 1798 when the Navy Department was created. Considerably later, in 1947, the Department of Defense was created to include the separate departments of the army, navy, and air force.

Although a few colonial-period military records can be found in the National Archives, the bulk of the military records there are of the men who served in the Revolutionary War and in succeeding wars. It has records from the Revolutionary War, the War of 1812, the Indian Wars (some Indians served on the side of the United States), the Mexican War, the Civil War (Union and some Confederate), the Spanish-American War, and the Philippine Insurrection. Only the records of those whose military service ended more than 75 years ago are open to the public.

The two types of service records maintained in the archives are those that pertain to military service and those that pertain to veterans' benefits such as pensions and land bounty warrants. In order to use these records effectively, one needs to know what branch of the service the ancestor was in, the state served from, the dates of service, and whether he was an officer or enlisted man. A further problem in researching military records is that in the early days of the United States it was permissible for a young man who was conscripted to supply a substitute to take his place. His replacement's only requirement was that he answer to the name of the soldier for whom he was substituting. The military apparently saw nothing improper about this practice as long as an able-bodied individual replaced the conscripted one. They did not realize what the ramifications of such an activity might have on future veteran benefits. After Congress passed various acts benefiting servicemen, it became apparent that proof of military service would be quite unobtainable for some veterans who had served their time only as substitutes. What made it even more difficult was the fact that many of these federal acts concerning veterans' benefits were passed decades after a particular war had been fought. By that time, the veterans were usually quite elderly or deceased as were most of the required witnesses to their military service. Later legislation changed this practice of military substitution.

Pension records are a much more informative source of information for the researcher than the military service records. This is because the applicant had to furnish considerable proof of his service time in the military. Three types of pensions were provided by the federal government: disability pensions for service-incurred injuries; pensions for specific periods of time served; and widows' pensions for wives and children whose husbands or fathers had been killed in service. Pension records contain such information

L | 147 | Ohio N. G.

William Lane

........., Co. F, 147 Reg't Ohio National Guard Inf.

Appears on

Company Descriptive Book

of the organization named above.

DESCRIPTION.

Age 23 years; height 5 feet 8 inches.

Complexion Dark

Eyes *Hazel* ; hair Blk

Where born Miami Co Ohio

Occupation Farmer

ENLISTMENT.

When May 2, 1864.

Where Camp Dennison, O.

By whom Gov of Ohio ; term 100 days

Remarks:

*as on book

(363g) Copyist.

L | 147 | Ohio N. G.

William Lane

Pvt., Co. F, 147 Reg't Ohio National Guard Inf.

Age 23 years.

Appears on Co. Muster-out Roll, dated

Camp Dennison O., Aug 30, 1864.

Muster-out to date Aug 30, 1864.

Last paid to Never Paid, 186 .

Clothing account:

Last settled........., 186 ; drawn since $......100

Due soldier $........100; due U. S. $........100

Am't for cloth'g in kind or money adv'd $ 18 42/100

Due U. S. for arms, equipments, &c., $........100

Bounty paid $........100; due $........100

Remarks:

Book mark:

F H Hall

(361) Copyist.

Figure 16a: Military Service Records

L | 147 | Ohio N. G.

William Lane

Pvt, Co. F, 147 Reg't Ohio National Guard Inf.

Appears on

Company Muster Roll

for May 16 to June 30, 1864.

Present or absent Present

Stoppage $ 100 for

Due Gov't $ 100 for

Remarks:

Book mark:

F. H. Hall

(858) Copyist.

L | 147 | Ohio N. G.

William McK. Lane

Pvt, Co. F, 147 Reg't Ohio National Guard Infantry.

Appears on

Company Muster and Descriptive Roll

of the organization named above. Roll dated

Camp Dennison May 16, 1864.

Where born Miami Co. O.

Age 23 y'rs; occupation Farmer

When enlisted May 2, 1864.*

Where enlisted Conover, O.*

For what period enlisted 100 days.*

Eyes Black; hair Black

Complexion Dark; height 5 ft. 8 in.

When mustered in May 16, 1864.

Muster-in to date May 16, 1864.

Where mustered in Camp Dennison

Bounty paid, $ 100; due, $ 100

Where credited

Company to which assigned

Remarks:

* Muster and descriptive, muster and muster-out rolls show enrollment of all men of this company as of same date.

Book mark:

F. H. Hall

(866d) Copyist.

Figure 16b: Military Service Records

about the veteran including his name, rank, military unit, period of service, residence, birthplace, and date of birth. A widow's pension record indicates further personal information about her and her children.

Other military records include bounty land warrants, bonuses of public land given out by the federal government for service in the Revolutionary War, the War of 1812, Indian Wars, and the Mexican War. These provide much of the same information as pension records as well as the number of acres granted and the date of granting. Most of the bounty warrants were sold to others since the veterans usually chose to remain in their old homestead. If the veteran died before the land was granted, then the record will also name his heirs who eventually received the land warrants instead.

A free booklet, *Military Service Records in the National Archives of the United States,* tells how to obtain copies of its military records and the proper forms to use. It can be obtained by writing to the National Archives General Service Administration, Washington, D.C. 20408. This booklet and other useful literature concerning genealogical research of the records of the federal government can also be found at the eleven archives branches listed in the appendix.

Although the records of more recent military activities are somewhat restricted as to public review, a certain amount of research is permitted under specific circumstances. Requests from a limited number of the veteran's immediate family can be honored in special cases.

As to military records located elsewhere, the National Society of the Daughters of the American Revolution library in Washington, D.C., has information on military payrolls of the Revolutionary War as well as pension records and bounty land warrant applications for that war. Many of the various state historical societies also have military records including those of the men who fought from that state on the side of the Confederacy during the Civil War. These men were not given pensions by the federal government, but certain states awarded pensions to those of its residents who served in the Confederate Army. Most genealogical libraries also have some records of past military service for the men who served in all of the various wars in which the United States participated.

WAR WITH Great Britton OF 1812.

DECLARATION OF A WIDOW FOR PENSION.

STATE OF Texas }
COUNTY OF Lamar } ss.

On this 8 day of June, A. D. 1878, personally appeared before me, Clerk of the County Court, a Court of record in and for the County and State aforesaid, Charlotta Rodgers, aged Eighty two years; a resident of the County of Lamar and State of Texas, who being duly sworn according to law, declares that she is the widow of William Rodgers who served the full period of sixty days in the military service of the United States, in the war with Great Britton of 1812., and who was the identical William Rodgers who (1) was inlisted, or drafted in Co. , commanded by Capt. Barnes, of Tennessee Mil. Inf Regiment, ——— Brigade, Gen David Carroll Division, at Murfeesburro Tenn, on (or about) the 20th day of Sept 1814, and was honorably discharged at New Orleans, La., on (or about) the 10th day of March 1815 (2) that he was Orderly Sergean of the above said Co of Capt Barnes, Tennessee Infantry, and marched with his said Co. to New Orleans and there participated in the Battle of the 8th of Jan 1815.

that she was married under the name of Charlotta Jackson to said William Rodgers on the 31st day of March 1814, by at there being no legal barrier to such marriage; that her said husband died at Columbia Co. Ark on the 21st day of July, — 1866. and that she has not re-married since his death; that she is not in receipt of a pension under any previous act; that she makes this declaration for the purpose of being placed on the pension rolls of the United States, under the provision of the act approved Feb 14th 1871, and hereby constitutes, and appoints, with full power of substitution and revocation, ~~[illegible]~~ her true and lawful attorney to prosecute her claim and obtain the pension certificate that may be issued; that her post-office is at Paris ———, in the County of Lamar and State of Texas ——, that her domicil or place of abode is ~~Paris~~, Lamar County Texas, ——

ATTEST:
Ed Gibbons
D. R. Rogers

Charlotta her x mark Rodgers,
APPLICANT.

NOTE—1. "Was drafted," "enlisted" or "volunteered."
" 2. Here give place, capacity and manner of service and any historical event in the war in which he participated.
NOTE.—That this declaration must be executed before a Clerk of a Court having a seal."

Figure 17: Declaration of a Widow for Pension

ORDER FOR COPIES OF VETERANS RECORDS
Please see Page 1 of this form for instructions.

Date Received (NNMS)

1. TYPE OF RECORD DESIRED (*We will search only one record per form*) ☐ PENSION ☐ BOUNTY-LAND WARRANT APPLICATION (*Service before 1856 only*) ☐ MILITARY

REQUIRED MINIMUM IDENTIFICATION OF VETERAN *Items 2, 3, 4, 5 (and 6 when applicable) MUST be completed or your order cannot be serviced.*	2 VETERAN (*Give last, first, and middle names*)		3 BRANCH OF SERVICE IN WHICH HE SERVED ☐ Army ☐ Navy ☐ Marine Corps
	4 STATE FROM WHICH SERVED	5 WAR IN WHICH, OR DATES BETWEEN WHICH, HE SERVED	6 IF SERVICE WAS CIVIL WAR ☐ Union ☐ Confederate

PLEASE PROVIDE THE FOLLOWING INFORMATION, IF KNOWN

7 UNIT IN WHICH HE SERVED (*Name of regiment or number, company, etc., name of ship*)		8 IF SERVICE WAS ARMY, ARM IN WHICH HE SERVED ☐ Infantry ☐ Cavalry ☐ Artillery	*If other, specify*	9 KIND OF SERVICE ☐ Volunteers ☐ Regulars
		10 PENSION/BOUNTY-LAND FILE NO	11 IF VETERAN LIVED IN A HOME FOR SOLDIERS, GIVE LOCATION (*City & State*)	12 PLACE(S) VETERAN LIVED AFTER SERVICE
13 DATE OF BIRTH	14 PLACE OF BIRTH (*City, County, State, etc.*)			
15 DATE OF DEATH	16 PLACE OF DEATH (*City, County, State, etc.*)		17 NAME OF WIDOW OR OTHER CLAIMANT	

Do NOT write below — Space is for our reply to you

☐ YES We have located the file you requested above.

We have copied all or part of the file for you. Make your check or money order for $ payable to **NATIONAL ARCHIVES TRUST FUND (NNMS).** Do NOT send cash. **Return your payment AND this invoice in the enclosed envelope. If the return envelope is missing, send your payment AND this invoice to: Cashier (NJC), National Archives Trust Fund, 8th and Pennsylvania Avenue, NW, Washington, DC 20408.** We must have this invoice to match your payment with your copies. WE WILL HOLD THESE COPIES AWAITING RECEIPT OF PAYMENT FOR 30 DAYS ONLY, FROM DATE STAMPED BELOW.

☐ NO We were unable to locate the file you requested above. See Below.

☐ **REQUIRED MINIMUM IDENTIFICATION OF VETERAN WAS NOT PROVIDED.** Please complete items 2 (give full name), 3, 4, 5, and 6, and resubmit your order.

☐ **A SEARCH WAS MADE BUT THE FILE YOU REQUESTED ABOVE WAS NOT FOUND.** When we do not find a record for a veteran, this does not mean that he did not serve. You may be able to obtain information about him from the archives of the State from which he served.

☐ See attached forms, leaflets, or information sheets.

SEARCHER	DATE	18 YOUR NAME AND ADDRESS
FILE DESIGNATION		

A

▶ *Print or type your name and address within the block below*

NAME (*Last, first, middle*)

STREET

CITY STATE (*Zip Code*)

NATIONAL ARCHIVES TRUST FUND BOARD
NATF Form 80 (1-84)

INVOICE/REPLY

ORDER FOR COPIES OF VETERANS RECORDS

INSTRUCTIONS FOR COMPLETING THIS FORM

Submit a separate set of forms for each file you request (see Item 1). **WE WILL SEARCH ONLY ONE RECORD PER FORM.** When you send more than one form at a time, each form may be handled separately. Therefore, you may not receive all of your replies at the same time. Remove this instruction sheet. Do NOT remove any of the remaining three pages of this form. Mail the completed form to:

Military Service Branch (NNMS)
National Archives and Records Service
8th and Pennsylvania Avenue, NW
Washington, DC 20408

DO NOT FORWARD PAYMENT WHEN SUBMITTING THIS FORM FOR SEARCH. When we search your order, photocopies will be made of records that relate to your request. At that time we will inform you of the cost to obtain these copies. **WE WILL HOLD THESE COPIES AWAITING RECEIPT OF PAYMENT FOR 30 DAYS ONLY.** After that time you must submit another form to obtain photocopies of the file.

NATF Form 80 replaces all prior versions of this form. **DO NOT SUBMIT PRIOR VERSIONS OF THIS FORM TO OBTAIN COPIES OF VETERANS RECORDS.**

DUE TO THE HEAVY VOLUME OF REQUESTS, PLEASE ALLOW A MINIMUM OF 8-10 WEEKS FOR PROCESSING OF YOUR ORDER.

Do NOT use this form to request photocopies of records relating to service in World War I or II, or subsequent service. Write to: National Personnel Records Center (Military Records), GSA, 9700 Page Boulevard, St. Louis, MO 63132.

IMPORTANT INFORMATION ABOUT YOUR ORDER

When, because of the size of a pension or bounty-land warrant application file, we are unable to provide copies of all documents, we will send copies of the documents we think will be most useful to you. You may order copies of all documents in a file by making a specific request. We will notify you of the cost of the copies.

Often there are many files for veterans of the same or nearly the same name. If there are **five or fewer files** for men with the same name as the individual in whom you are interested, we will examine all the relevant files and compare their contents with the information that you have provided us. If the veteran's identity seems obvious, we will furnish you a copy of the file we think is the correct one.

If there are more than five files, we will not make a file-by-file check to see if the information in the numerous files matches that provided for the veteran in whom you are interested. In such cases, we suggest that you visit the National Archives and examine the various files, or hire a professional researcher to examine the files for you. We do not maintain a list of persons who do research for a fee; however, many researchers advertise their services in genealogical periodicals, usually available in libraries.

Additional copies of this form and more information about the availability of records pertaining to military service or family histories may be found in our free genealogical information leaflets and forms. These may be requested by writing to:

Reference Services Branch (NNIR)
National Archives and Records Service
8th and Pennsylvania Avenue, NW
Washington, DC 20408

PLEASE SEE THE REVERSE OF THIS PAGE FOR THE TYPES OF RECORDS THAT CAN BE ORDERED WITH THIS FORM.

NATIONAL ARCHIVES TRUST FUND BOARD — **INSTRUCTIONS** — NATF Form 80 (1-84)

Figure 18: Order for Copies of Veterans Records

CHAPTER 12

Computer Genealogy

> People can be divided into three groups: those who make things happen, those who watch things happen, and those who wonder what happened.
>
> —JOHN W. NEWBERN

Computerized genealogy; is it for you? Today we are living in an age of computers and like it or not, they are here to stay. Computers function well in handling not only the routine, monotonous jobs, but also the most difficult and complex operations, all with the most apparent ease. They can increase productivity and expedite paperwork by compressing hours of human labor into seconds of computer time and print it out, all in the wink of an eye. And they can help you compose, edit, and print out that important letter or document without the tedious rewriting or retyping so often required when using an ordinary typewriter, leaving you free for more creative activities.

And now computers have invaded the time-honored field of genealogical research, a discipline traditionally known for its slow, methodical, and painstaking fact-finding. Can anything so high tech be of benefit to you personally? Will it be worth your while to invest the money, time, and dedication required to successfully computerize your own family record collection? And in the long run, will the benefits outweigh any perceived disadvantages of computerization?

The advantages can be legion. Genealogy, with its emphasis on not only the compilation of statistical data and family history, but the interpretation, analysis, and explanation of source material, can be the perfect science for a computerization program. As a side benefit, computer genealogy offers an efficient record management system because it forces you to be more uniform and consistent in your data recording. In order for a computer to effectively edit or update entries, it must know exactly where the records are and in what form.

Computerization also provides a new medium of data exchange for genealogists. Computerized family information can be traded with other genealogists either by mailed diskettes or by use of a modem, a device that communicates through telephone lines with other computers. And instant printouts of all of your pedigree forms can be produced immediately for mailing out, publishing, or merely filing away for future reference.

Because you utilize for the most part a standard keyboard, if you wish you can start writing your family history from the time you begin entering the data into the computer's memory system. You don't even need to be a good typist. Corrections are easily made and blocks of text can be edited and moved to suit any format you desire. And footnotes and source material identification, so important to a valid genealogy, can be referenced and documented continuously as you work.

The computer is especially adept at performing repetitious tasks. If, for example, your family's data collection reflects the same surnames and place names over and over again and chances are it will, writing all of these names and places can be tedious drudgery. If your computer has specially designed "function" keys sometimes indicated by the "F" symbol, as in "F 1," "F 2," or "F 3," they can be programmed to avoid repetitious retyping by assigning each of these keys to a particular surname or location. Thus "F 1" could become, for example, "Underwood" or any name of your choice, and "F 2" could stand for say, "Sacramento County, California" or, of course, any other location that you chose. In some computers, other combinations of numbers or letters produce the same result.

There can be, of course, certain drawbacks to computerizing your genealogy collections. The first and most readily apparent is the cost factor. Although computer hardware has greatly decreased in price in the last few years, an adequate system could still run into considerable expense. This system should include a computer with a sufficient memory capacity capable of handling your specific program, a monitor or screen that displays at least 80 characters per line with 24 lines, a typewriter-type keyboard, two disk drives, either built-in or external, and a printer necessary to print out your charts and family history. Other items you may need to include are a modem, interface cables for connecting the computer to its peripheral items, and a computer table, all items that can add up to a sizable investment.

Another apparent drawback to computerizing your genealogy collection can be learning to operate a computer system. The thought of this can be intimidating and threatening especially for those of us who grew up in a noncomputerized world. Listening to a conversation between two computer buffs sometimes produces the same feeling of bewilderment one experiences in a foreign land, with the conviction that one will never learn the language. But the same attributes that led you up the genealogical path in the first place can serve you in good stead at this point, namely, patience and perseverance. A comprehensive study of your computer's user's manual and hands-on practice on your machine should do the rest.

Even after you have acquired the computer system and the necessary technological skills needed to launch yourself into the world of computerized genealogy, there is still the tedious task of feeding all of your family history into the machine's memory system. Fortunately, this inputting only has to be done once. From then on, your computer is your servant, not your master, responding to your every command, assuming, of course, that the commands are issued in correct computerese.

But there are a few caveats here also. The data is usually fed into the computer's memory by way of a floppy diskette, or disk as it is known. Care must be taken with it as disks are very sensitive to external conditions, especially heat and cold, and even smoke can affect them. Disks must always be handled particularly carefully even when labeling as they are also sensitive to pressure. If your disk is exposed to a magnet, its memory can be lost forever. For example, exposure to an airport checkpoint can destroy a disk's memory completely. Unfortunately, one cannot always anticipate when a device containing a magnet is on the premises so the best protection is to have at least two backup disks in case one is lost.

Another occasion in which you could lose all of your input data in your computer's RAM, its temporary memory, is if there is a sudden power failure before you get a chance to officially store the material into one of its disks. If, for example, you should wander off to the kitchen for a ham sandwich without first signaling the computer to "file" the data, you may return to find yourself confronted with an empty monitor screen, a sign that your program has "crashed," computer language for the loss of a program before it is officially stored. So always try to file the material two or three times an hour while operating your machine.

Notwithstanding some of the above-mentioned disadvantages of computerization, it has much to offer a dedicated genealogist. Once your database, that is, your store of usable genealogical information is created, the retrieval of family data and the printing out of family group sheets and pedigree charts can be easy and fun. The amateur as well as the professional genealogist can benefit from the efficient record management system, telecommunications, and the word processing functions that a computer system can provide.

For the sake of those who do not own a computer, there are a few basic terms that are common to most systems. The machine, itself, is called "hardware," a term that includes also anything factory-attached to it, such as the screen, keyboard, and the disk drives, if they are all in one cabinet. If any of these components which are used for the input or output of data from the computer are separate from the computer they are called "peripherals" and must be connected to the machine by way of interface devices. These devices, also known as "ports," are either "serial" or "parallel" and must match the computer component connected to it.

The brain of the computer system is the central processing unit, or "CPU." The CPU, in which resides a silicone chip—the microprocessor—controls the operation of the computer's disk drives and printer as well as the flow of data in the system. It also performs various decision-making functions and interprets instructions to the computer's other components as it receives them.

Located in the CPU are the "bits"—a term that stands for "binary digits" and refers to the elements that govern a computer's speed and power, somewhat as a car's cylinders would do. Although the most basic piece of information a computer can handle, the bit is also one of the most important as the "bit size" of a computer determines its memory capacity and speed of operation.

A group of 8 bits is called a "byte." A byte is used for one character, which to the computer can mean a letter, a number, a punctuation mark, or a space. A computer's memory is usually referred to by the letter "K" standing for "kilobyte" and equaling 1,024 bytes, but generally rounded off to 1,000. Thus a computer with a memory of 64,000 bytes would be referred to as having a memory capacity of 64K. Once this was considered extensive, but today many computer systems have the capability of expanding their memory system to "megabytes" or "M" of RAM, each of which is over 1 million bytes or 1,024K bytes.

The memory of a computer system consists of two types, internal and external. The first, the internal memory, is built into the machine itself and is also divided into two types—ROM, which stands for "read-only memory," and RAM, which means "random-access memory." In the ROM can be found a computer's instructions to the user, which cannot be altered, added to, or lost. It is described as "non-volatile" and is permanently in the computer's memory and used for specific, often used programs. Some ROMs contain other information such as a basic language for use with the computer.

The second part of the internal memory, the RAM, is the part of the computer into which you temporarily input your data before storing into the machine's external memory. RAM's memory is "volatile," which means it will go away if the power is lost or the machine is turned off before the command is given to store the data. It is the RAM size that is referred to when a computer is described as "64K" or "128K." One might think that a computer with 64,000 bytes might be adequate for most anything; however, most genealogical programs today call for a much larger RAM capacity.

How does one protect and store this volatile, unstable data that sits so precariously in your computer's RAM? This is where the computer's second memory type, the external, comes in.

External memory is another name for a computer's mass storage system, a place in which data and programs are stored for later use. It is your computer's filing system. This storage system is vital because it generally has a greater capacity than your machine's internal RAM, can supply data upon command, and is non-volatile, meaning the information remains in its memory even when the machine is turned off.

A floppy disk is the storage device utilized by most computer users. It looks like a little 45 rpm record and comes in three sizes—a 3-inch, a 5¼-inch, and an 8-inch diameter. The disk is not floppy, but is actually a thin piece of mylar inside a paper jacket. It can be a "single" or "double density" and a "single" or "double-sided" disk. A double-density, double-sided disk can store the most data and some floppy disks can hold many kilobytes or even megabytes of memory.

A floppy disk drive, the device that holds the disk, is a rotating magnetic recording medium with a read/write head. Because the head can feed into or extract the recorded data from any portion of the disk, it is referred to as "random-access," as any piece of information can be retrieved from the disk upon command.

You will need two floppy disk drives, one for using the current program and the other to safely store it. In the case of built-in drives, you will have to remember which disk drive you are using for what purpose. To help remember, the system or program disk should be placed in the first position drive and your data disk placed in the other. And when you are through with the day's session always remember to use the proper phrase, whatever it is, to "file" the data before you power down, otherwise your previous input data will crash before you can store it.

If your program is extensive and you have much data to store, you may want to consider a hard disk drive. A hard disk drive can store up to many megabytes of information, that is, millions of characters more than can usually be stored on a floppy disk. You will still need to utilize at least one floppy disk drive to effectively use a word processor or other genealogy program. Hard disk drives are quite expensive and not every computer can be adapted to one. The disk, known as a "platter," is not removable and is sealed in its drive at all times. Hard disks not only have a greater storage capacity, they transfer information much faster than the floppy disk drives. However, if you do not need the additional storage, you may find that the expense may not justify the purchase of a hard disk at this time.

In regard to other computer data storage methods, one of the most innovative concepts to appear in the computer marketplace lately has been a shiny compact laser disk called CD-ROM. First cousin to the compact disk that revolutionized the music market's audio technology, CD-ROM stands for Compact Disk Read-Only Memory. Functioning much like the ROM of your computer, you can read from it, but you cannot add to or delete from it. Purchased with the desired information already on it, a CD-ROM disk is intended as a reference source only, storing as it can, up to 550,000,000 bytes of information, or thousands of times more characters than can a traditional floppy disk.

The advantages of CD-ROM are legion. For example, one can purchase CD-ROMs containing certain database collections from computerized genealogical libraries such as Automated Archives, Inc., or from Everton Publishers' Computerized Roots Cellar, a database of events submitted by their customers. The LDS Church has already made its three huge database collections—the Ancestral File, the International Genealogical Index, and its Family History Library—available for access at the LDS Library at Salt Lake City. There are also many other genealogical collections now being readied or are already available for purchase or access, with more being planned.

As innovative and useful as this new reference source system is, it does, however, have one major drawback, and that is its cost. The required laser disk player, which your computer treats as another disk drive, is quite expensive, as are the CD-ROMs themselves. They are, however, coming down in price as more and more database collection operators are supplying new and unique source material for the CD-ROMs.

Other peripheral items of importance for a computer system are the video monitor or screen and the keyboard. Together they are known as a "terminal." Terminals are the primary communication devices between the user and the computer. Information typed on the keyboard passes directly into the computer where it is received and flashed back to the monitor for viewing. This tells you the machine has received the information. The rate of speed at which this information is transmitted is called the "baud rate."

The monitor should measure at least 12 inches diagonally and offer at least 80 characters per line with usually 24 lines. A color monitor is not necessary for a genealogy program, which generally consists of a word processing function combined with a data-base management program. Monochrome screens of green or amber are considered easiest on the eyes over a long period of time. Television screens are not effective monitors for use with computers as they can offer only 25 lines with about 40 characters per line, far too little for most genealogy software. Some genealogy programs require even wider screens than the standard 80 character size, although so far, they are not common.

The monitor's partner component, the keyboard, should be selected for comfort and ease of handling. Some keyboards are detachable from the monitor, which means that they can be adjusted for the user's comfort during the computing operation. Most of the keys resemble those of a standard typewriter, but there are some special ones, such as the escape and control keys used for unique computer combinations. Other special keys can include a standard 10-key adding machine function that is quite useful if a great amount of numeric data is to be fed into the computer's memory. There are cursor control keys also unique to computers that show the user where the next character is placed on the screen. These are sometimes indicated by four keys with little arrows on them indicating the directions of up, down, left and right that point to where the work was left off. Some computers have a little "mouse" instead, a hand-directed device that is rolled on the desk top to move the cursor arrow to the appropriate place on the screen.

Because genealogy is primarily a discipline of data collecting and recording, whatever else you buy, one of your most important investments should be a good printer. Every genealogist needs to produce many ancestral charts and pedigree forms to retain or to mail out to interested kinfolk. And of course, you may want to word process the family genealogy in hopes of someday publishing that important book, your family history. Another useful function of a good printer is the ability to print out mailing lists for family correspondence, a valuable asset to some genealogists.

For genealogical purposes, the two most popular printer types at present are letter quality and dot matrix. They are called "impact" printers because, in both cases, the letter is formed by the striking of a character against a ribbon, making an impression on paper. There are also "non-impact" types, such as the thermal, ink jet, and the more costly laser printer, but so far they are not used as much as the impact ones for reasons of cost and utility.

Letter quality printers resemble typewriter type and, in fact, some typewriters are designed to also serve as computer printers. This is not a good idea as most typewriters are not constructed for such heavy duty use. It is better to invest in a good letter quality or dot matrix printer, or both, if you can afford them. Letter quality printers utilize either a daisy wheel or a thimble type element. Both of these elements come with interchangeable wheels, meaning the type fonts can be changed at will. Because it has the most attractive type, word processing is usually done on a letter quality printer. The print wheels are not durable, however, as a character can snap off at any time, so one should have at least one or two backup wheels in case of emergency.

Dot matrix printers form their characters by the use of groups of needlelike pins shaped into letters called print heads. When a print head strikes an inked ribbon, it produces a pattern of dots on the paper in the form of a letter. The less expensive a matrix printer, the fewer dots are used for the letters and the more difficult the type is to read. Because of its speed, a dot matrix printer can be used most successfully for rough drafts, bills, and invoices, and for printing out reduced-size pedigree charts and forms.

Certain genealogy programs require specialized printing functions. For instance, the Church of the Latter Day Saints in Salt Lake City, indicates in the brochures for its genealogy program *Personal Ancestral File,* that printers equipped with either a dot matrix's compressed print of 17 characters per inch or a letter perfect elite print of 12 pitch or characters per line are required for all of its genealogy software versions. A few other genealogy programs also call for up to 132 printed characters per line instead of the usual 80 or 90 characters.

These requirements are necessary because certain genealogical forms to be printed out, such as a five or more generation pedigree chart, could exceed a standard 8½ x 11-inch width of paper. If you do not wish to invest in another printer, you might get by using a standard legal size sheet sideways and printing the chart on its long 14-inch side, assuming your printer has this capability. If you have many oversized forms, however, perhaps a dot matrix printer with a compressed type mode may be your answer.

An important capability of a good printing system is the effective handling of the paper being processed. There are several different ways of feeding paper through a printer. The most common and the one most printers furnish, is by friction feed such as typewriters use. In this method, the paper is squeezed between two platens or rollers, which move it through the printer. This type of feed is convenient because it uses all sizes of paper including letterhead bond and envelopes. Its disadvantage is that with friction feed, the long continuous forms that some genealogists use may not move along precisely and evenly and can easily get out of alignment.

A more effective paper handling accessory is a tractor feed, which is designed to move special continuous-form paper through the printer. This is done with a tread-like attachment that applies several sprockets to the holes in the edge of the paper to move it along. After printing, the perforated edges of the paper are torn away and the sheets separated, making them look like ordinary 8½ x 11-inch paper. This method is particularly useful for genealogy programs requiring unusual or oversized family ancestral charts or forms.

Up to now we have covered only the basic necessary components of an effective computer system. There is, however, one peripheral item that would be useful to a computer genealogist, if not now then down the road. This device is called a "modem," short for "modular-demodular." A modem is connected to your computer and translates computer data into audible tones for transmission over telephone lines to a receiving modem. The answering modem then converts the audible tones back to computer signals for reception by its own computer or terminal. Modems are connected to phone lines in two ways, with acoustic couplers placed on the telephone or by direct wire connection that bypasses the telephone and connects directly to the telephone lines. Of the two methods, the direct connect modem has the highest "baud rate," that is, is the speediest. Speed of transmission is important as it saves on phone bills when transmitting through long distance lines. This type of transmission is called "telecommunications."

What is the advantage to a genealogist in having a modem? A modem can be an excellent method of obtaining information from other genealogical databases or ancestral collections. You can even hook up to a computer with a database collection in another city, if you desire. At present, linking personal database systems together is limited to the confines of your own family lines or to some private commercial database collection. However, it is hoped that in the near future by using a modem and your computer, you may be able to add to or retrieve family information from a giant genealogy database system such as the one being developed by the LDS Church in Salt Lake City. When this happens, the contents of LDS's Genealogical Library will afford a computer genealogist access to a vast universal family file of information limited only by his computer's memory capacity.

So far, we have discussed only the computer, its peripheral component and its interface devices. But a computer, itself, is nothing; it is the software—the programs that give it character, personality, and life. A computer alone is like a phonograph player without records; it produces no music. It is up to the user to supply the missing ingredients, in your case, effective genealogy software.

Computer software comes in three general types: system software, programming language, and applications software. All three are required for an effective software program. System software is the tool that tells the computer how to run its disk operating system, known as its "DOS." The DOS, responding to the user's commands, directs the flow of data around the computer, moves the data on and off the disk drives, and operates the printer. It is what is referred to when a system is described as "CP/M" or "MS-DOS." It is also the factor that determines what applications software will run on your machine.

All computer programs are written in a programming language, which is a set of instructions that tells your computer what to do. Most computers have a BASIC language, standing for Beginners All Purpose Symbolic Instruction Code, which is adapted for use with the computer and usually included with it as part of the package. BASIC and other programs are designed for those who wish to program their own computers. It is not required for operating applications programs that are already written in their own programming language.

The third type of software is the applications programs, which are what most people are concerned with when they talk of software. An applications program combined with programming language and a system program allows the user to do certain jobs such as word processing, spelling checking, and inventory control. For a genealogist, this could also include such functions as a record management program and printing out indexes and ancestral forms and charts.

Although a good basic genealogy applications program could be considered an effective database management system combined with a word processing function, some genealogists prefer to work with word processing programs exclusively rather than with a specific genealogy program. The simplicity of the word processing operation, the ease in which corrections are made, and the ability to create mailing lists are all important functions for genealogists. And if writing and publishing your family history is also one of your future goals, then a word processor's ability to edit and store relevant information for future updating can be a godsend.

But if documenting and storing ancestral data such as births, deaths, and marriages is of equal importance, you will be interested in a genealogy program that offers, in addition, a good database management function with an effective retrieval system. Genealogy programs can also store information on family relationships, offspring, occupations, and other relevant biographical data for each ancestor. This storage can be searched, arranged, and retrieved in index form or any other classification your program can produce.

Your ancestral charts and family group sheets can be printed out in a variety of ways as each genealogy program's forms seem to vary a little in format and sophistication. But a basic function of good genealogy software should be the ability to duplicate the classic, standard, preprinted charts and forms found in the retail stores. Furthermore, once your family data is properly entered in the computer, your program should be able to print out any number of different family trees and charts linking all of your ancestors together. These forms should include pedigree charts, both ascending and descending, individual and group sheets, and various types of indexes.

Some of the following displayed computer printouts offer a random sampling of a few of the forms utilized by the different genealogy programs in the marketplace and are presented to show the variations between them. The first form indicated is a family group sheet (Figure 19) from *Your Family Tree,* Hurdware, Inc., a program designed for the Commodore 64 and the IBM PCs. From *Genealogical Data Base Systems* by Data Base Systems, is a descendant chart and an Ahnentafel or direct line chart (Figure 20) designed for the Apple II Computer family. Valley Software's *The Family Tree Genealogy System* offers a data collection form (Figure 21) and a family chart disk (Figure 22) from its genealogy software for IBM and compatible machines.

GROUP SHEET FOR:	Reeks	Mary Willie	(3)
SPOUSE:	Hurd	Elbert Eugene "Jack"	(2)
FATHER:	Reeks	Robert Melvin	(6)
MOTHER:	Ragsdale	Lelia May	(7)
CHILD	Hurd	John William	(1)
DATE OF BIRTH:	03/30/1903		
PLACE OF BIRTH:	TN Trimble		
DATE OF MARRIAGE:	11/26/1924		
PLACE OF MARRIAGE:	TN Memphis		
DATE OF DEATH:	04/29/1964		
PLACE OF DEATH:	TN Memphis		
REMARKS:	Orphan at 16; supported bro & 2 sis. Widow at 29; raised five children alone.		
BROTHERS AND SISTERS:	Reeks	John Samuel	(3.1)
	Reeks	Sarah Louise	(3.2)
	Reeks	Lady Muriel	(3.3)
OTHER CHILDREN:	Hurd	Bobbie Jean	(1.1)
	Hurd	Jo Eva	(1.2)
	Hurd	Billie Louise	(1.3)
	Hurd	Walker Reeks	(1.4)

Figure 19: Family Group Sheet
(from Your Family Tree. *Courtesy Hurdware, Inc.)*

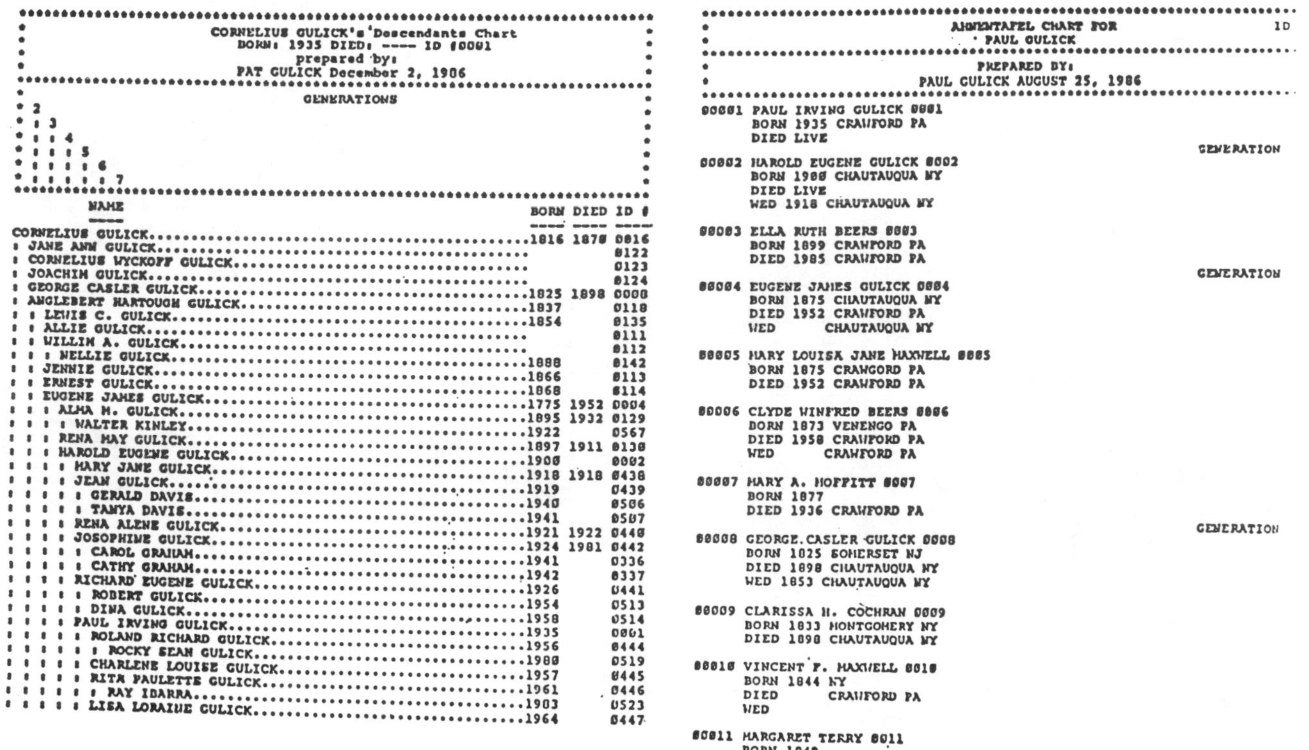

```
CORNELIUS GULICK's Descendants Chart
BORN: 1935 DIED: ---- ID #0001
prepared by:
PAT GULICK December 2, 1986
GENERATIONS
: 2
: : 3
: : : 4
: : : : 5
: : : : : 6
: : : : : : 7
NAME                                         BORN DIED ID #
----                                         ---- ---- ----
CORNELIUS GULICK.............................1816 1870 0016
: JANE ANN GULICK...................................... 0122
: CORNELIUS WYCKOFF GULICK............................. 0123
: JOACHIM GULICK....................................... 0124
: GEORGE CASLER GULICK.......................1825 1898 0008
: ANGLEBERT HARTOUGH GULICK..................1837      0118
: : LEWIS C. GULICK..........................1854      0135
: : ALLIE GULICK....................................... 0111
: : WILLIM A. GULICK................................... 0112
: : : NELLIE GULICK............................1888      0142
: : JENNIE GULICK............................1866      0113
: : ERNEST GULICK............................1868      0114
: : EUGENE JAMES GULICK......................1775 1952 0004
: : : ALMA M. GULICK.........................1895 1932 0129
: : : : WALTER KINLEY..........................1922      0567
: : : RENA MAY GULICK........................1897 1911 0130
: : : HAROLD EUGENE GULICK...................1900      0002
: : : : MARY JANE GULICK.......................1918 1918 0438
: : : : JEAN GULICK............................1919      0439
: : : : : GERALD DAVIS.........................1940      0506
: : : : : TANYA DAVIS..........................1941      0507
: : : : RENA ALENE GULICK......................1921 1922 0440
: : : : JOSOPHINE GULICK.......................1924 1981 0442
: : : : : CAROL GRAHAM.........................1941      0336
: : : : : CATHY GRAHAM.........................1942      0337
: : : : RICHARD EUGENE GULICK..................1926      0441
: : : : : ROBERT GULICK........................1954      0513
: : : : : DINA GULICK..........................1958      0514
: : : : PAUL IRVING GULICK.....................1935      0001
: : : : : ROLAND RICHARD GULICK................1956      0444
: : : : : : ROCKY SEAN GULICK..................1980      0519
: : : : : CHARLENE LOUISE GULICK...............1957      0445
: : : : : RITA PAULETTE GULICK.................1961      0446
: : : : : : RAY IBARRA.........................1903      0523
: : : : : LISA LORAINE GULICK..................1964      0447
```

```
AHNENTAFEL CHART FOR                                   ID
PAUL GULICK
PREPARED BY:
PAUL GULICK AUGUST 25, 1986

00001 PAUL IRVING GULICK 0001
      BORN 1935 CRAWFORD PA
      DIED LIVE
                                                GENERATION
00002 HAROLD EUGENE GULICK 0002
      BORN 1900 CHAUTAUQUA NY
      DIED LIVE
      WED 1918 CHAUTAUQUA NY

00003 ELLA RUTH BEERS 0003
      BORN 1899 CRAWFORD PA
      DIED 1985 CRAWFORD PA
                                                GENERATION
00004 EUGENE JAMES GULICK 0004
      BORN 1875 CHAUTAUQUA NY
      DIED 1952 CRAWFORD PA
      WED       CHAUTAUQUA NY

00005 MARY LOUISA JANE MAXWELL 0005
      BORN 1875 CRAWGORD PA
      DIED 1952 CRAWFORD PA

00006 CLYDE WINFRED BEERS 0006
      BORN 1873 VENENGO PA
      DIED 1958 CRAWFORD PA
      WED       CRAWFORD PA

00007 MARY A. MOFFITT 0007
      BORN 1877
      DIED 1936 CRAWFORD PA
                                                GENERATION
00008 GEORGE CASLER GULICK 0008
      BORN 1825 SOMERSET NJ
      DIED 1898 CHAUTAUQUA NY
      WED 1853 CHAUTAUQUA NY

00009 CLARISSA H. COCHRAN 0009
      BORN 1833 MONTGOMERY NY
      DIED 1898 CHAUTAUQUA NY

00010 VINCENT F. MAXWELL 0010
      BORN 1844 NY
      DIED      CRAWFORD PA
      WED

00011 MARGARET TERRY 0011
      BORN 1849
      DIED
```

Figure 20: Descendant Chart and Ahnentafel Chart
(Data Base Systems, Genealogical Data Base Systems)

```
THE  FAMILY  TREE  GENEALOGY  SYSTEM
================== DATA COLLECTION FORM ===================
:                                                          :
:         KEY: ___                                         :
:         NAME: ______________________________             :
:         BORN: ________  BP: ____________________         :
:         CHR:  ________  CP: ____________________         :
:         WED:  ________  WP: ____________________         :
:         MIL:  ________  BR: ____________________         :
:         DIED: ________  DP: ____________________         :
:         BURY: ____________________  C:_______            :
:         OCC: ______________  RL:______________           :
:         COMMENTS:_______________________________         :
:         ________________________________________         :
:                                                          :
:================== PARENT-SPOUSE-DATA ==================:
:                                                          :
:         FA:____  N:______________________________        :
:         MO:____  N:______________________________        :
:         S1:____  N:______________________________        :
:         S2:____  N:______________________________        :
:         S3:____  N:______________________________        :
:                                                          :
:===================== THE CHILDREN =====================:
:         S CHLD S                 BIRTH     DEATH         :
:         # DKEY X CHILDS-NAME     DATE      DATE          :
:         _ ____ _ _____________ ________ ________         :
:         _ ____ _ _____________ ________ ________         :
:         _ ____ _ _____________ ________ ________         :
:         _ ____ _ _____________ ________ ________         :
:         _ ____ _ _____________ ________ ________         :
:         _ ____ _ _____________ ________ ________         :
:         _ ____ _ _____________ ________ ________         :
:         _ ____ _ _____________ ________ ________         :
:         _ ____ _ _____________ ________ ________         :
:         _ ____ _ _____________ ________ ________         :
:         _ ____ _ _____________ ________ ________         :
:         _ ____ _ _____________ ________ ________         :
:         _ ____ _ _____________ ________ ________         :
:         _ ____ _ _____________ ________ ________         :
:         _ ____ _ _____________ ________ ________         :
:==========================================================:
:===================== THE SOURCES ======================:
:                                                          :
:         ENTRY: ________  BY: ____________________        :
:         SOURCES:    ______________________________       :
:         ________________________________________         :
:         ________________________________________         :
:======================== LEGEND ========================:
:    BORN= BIRTH DATE                BP= PLACE OF BIRTH     :
:    CHR = CHRISTENING DATE          CP= CHRISTENING PLACE  :
:    WED = WEDDING DATE              WP= WEDDING PLACE      :
:    MIL = MILITARY DATE             BR= BRANCH/RANK        :
:    DIED= DEATH DATE                DP= DEATH PLACE        :
:    BURY= PLACE BURIED              C = CEMETARY           :
:    OCC = OCCUPATION                RL= RELIGIOUS PREF     :
:    FA  = FATHERS DISK & KEY        N = FATHERS NAME       :
:    MO  = MOTHERS DISK & KEY        N = MOTHERS NAME       :
:    S1  = SPOUSE 1 DISK & KEY       N = SPOUSE 1 NAME      :
:    CHLD-DKEY = CHILDS DISK & KEY SX= SEX OF CHILD         :
:         S#= THE SPOUSE NUMBER OF CHILDS PARENT            :
============================================================
```

Figure 21: Data Collection Form

(Valley Software, The Family Tree Genealogical System)

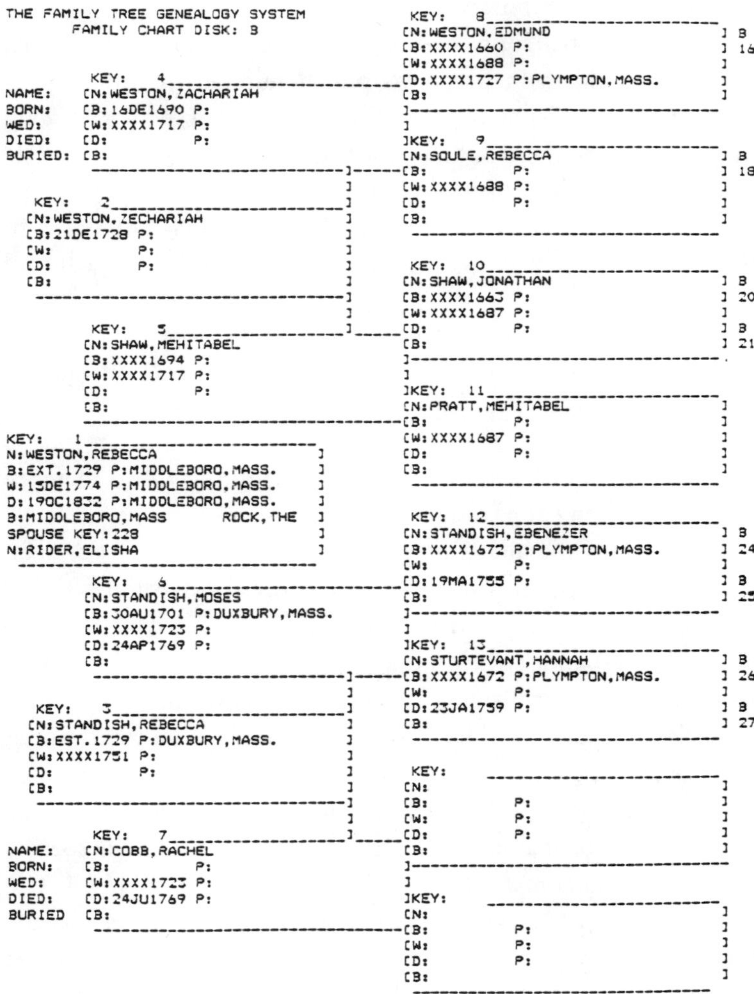

```
THE FAMILY TREE GENEALOGY SYSTEM                       KEY:   8__________________________
      FAMILY CHART DISK: B                             [N:WESTON,EDMUND                   ] B
                                                       [B:XXXX1660 P:                     ] 16
                                                       [W:XXXX1688 P:                     ]
         KEY:   4______________________________________[D:XXXX1727 P:PLYMPTON,MASS.      ]
NAME:    [N:WESTON,ZACHARIAH                           [B:                                ]
BORN:    [B:16DE1690 P:                                ]----------------------------------
WED:     [W:XXXX1717 P:                                ]
DIED:    [D:           P:                              ]KEY:   9_________________________
BURIED:  [B:                                           [N:SOULE,REBECCA                   ] B
         --------------------------]-----[B:           P:                                 ] 18
                                   ]                   [W:XXXX1688 P:                     ]
   KEY:   2________________________]                   [D:           P:                   ]
  [N:WESTON,ZECHARIAH              ]                   [B:                                ]
  [B:21DE1728 P:                   ]                   ----------------------------------
  [W:         P:                   ]
  [D:         P:                   ]                   KEY:  10__________________________
  [B:                              ]                   [N:SHAW,JONATHAN                   ] B
  ---------------------------------]                   [B:XXXX1663 P:                     ] 20
                                   ]                   [W:XXXX1687 P:                     ]
         KEY:   5__________________]_____[D:           P:                                 ] B
         [N:SHAW,MEHITABEL                             [B:                                ] 21
         [B:XXXX1694 P:                                ]----------------------------------
         [W:XXXX1717 P:                                ]
         [D:           P:                              ]KEY:  11_________________________
         [B:                                           [N:PRATT,MEHITABEL                 ]
         --------------------------------------------[B:           P:                     ]
KEY:   1_______________________                        [W:XXXX1687 P:                     ]
N:WESTON,REBECCA                   ]                   [D:           P:                   ]
B:EXT.1729 P:MIDDLEBORO,MASS.      ]                   [B:                                ]
W:15DE1774 P:MIDDLEBORO,MASS.      ]                   ----------------------------------
D:19OC1832 P:MIDDLEBORO,MASS.      ]
B:MIDDLEBORO,MASS        ROCK,THE  ]                   KEY:  12__________________________
SPOUSE KEY:228                     ]                   [N:STANDISH,EBENEZER               ] B
N:RIDER,ELISHA                     ]                   [B:XXXX1672 P:PLYMPTON,MASS.       ] 24
  ------------------------------                       [W:           P:                   ]
         KEY:   6______________________________________[D:19MA1755 P:                     ] B
         [N:STANDISH,MOSES                             [B:                                ] 25
         [B:30AU1701 P:DUXBURY,MASS.                   ]----------------------------------
         [W:XXXX1723 P:                                ]
         [D:24AP1769 P:                                ]KEY:  13_________________________
         [B:                                           [N:STURTEVANT,HANNAH               ] B
         --------------------------]-----[B:XXXX1672 P:PLYMPTON,MASS.                     ] 26
                                   ]                   [W:           P:                   ]
   KEY:   3________________________]                   [D:23JA1759 P:                     ] B
  [N:STANDISH,REBECCA              ]                   [B:                                ] 27
  [B:EST.1729 P:DUXBURY,MASS.      ]                   ----------------------------------
  [W:XXXX1751 P:                   ]
  [D:         P:                   ]                   KEY:        ______________________
  [B:                              ]                   [N:                                ]
  ---------------------------------]                   [B:           P:                   ]
                                   ]                   [W:           P:                   ]
         KEY:   7__________________]_____[D:           P:                                 ]
NAME:    [N:COBB,RACHEL                                [B:                                ]
BORN:    [B:           P:                              ]----------------------------------
WED:     [W:XXXX1723 P:                                ]
DIED:    [D:24JU1769 P:                                ]KEY:       ______________________
BURIED   [B:                                           [N:                                ]
         --------------------------------------------[B:           P:                     ]
                                                       [W:           P:                   ]
                                                       [D:           P:                   ]
                                                       [B:                                ]
                                                       ----------------------------------
```

Figure 22: Pedigree Chart

(Valley Software, The Family Tree Genealogical System)

Two of the most professional genealogical programs on the market today are *Roots II* and *Roots III,* produced by Commsoft. *Roots III,* introduced in 1988, is a greatly expanded and improved version of the already popular *Roots II,* which should make it the leading genealogy software package for IBM computers. Unfortunately, this excellent software is limited at present to IBMs and compatible computers only.

Another worthy software is *Family Roots,* from Quinsept, Inc., which offers six main programs plus a number of utility ones. *Family Roots* is available for computer systems that include, among others, the Apple IIs and the IBM PCs.

For Apple's Macintosh, there is a genealogy software package, *Family Heritage File,* a program somewhat similar to, but higher in price than LDS's *Personal Ancestral File*'s version for the Macintosh Computer.

For limited memory machines such as the Atari Computer, there is *Family History* from Direct Lines Software that offers a less extensive program requiring only 48K RAM. Another limited genealogy program is *The Genealogy Workshop* from Microsphere, Inc., designed for Texas Instrument T. I. 99/4A with a memory capacity requirement of only 32K.

Forms from the above programs include free-form pedigrees, compressed charts, individual sheets, predecessor charts and alphabetized or numerically indexed ancestral lists. Some of the programs have expanded their storage and retrieval capabilities with the addition of such things as pictures, maps, and plot plans. These last are usually done with help from the more advanced graphics programs.

There are also special purpose programs that do not handle family records or maintain research files, but instead have specific genealogical functions. One such program is *ANCS-U-LATOR,* from GEN-N-DEX, which can establish calendar dates for the day of the week for certain historical events, either past or future. It also offers a generation finder, a function that demonstrates relationship determination by showing how a common ancestor's descendants are related.

There are, of course, many other effective genealogy programs available today for almost any computer system. The above mentioned genealogy software was chosen as typical of some of them and the forms they offer as representative. This chapter does not attempt to review or analyze any specific software but intends only to point out some of the wide assortment of programs and forms on hand for computer genealogists.

There is, however, one genealogy software package that deserves special mention at this time, and that is *Personal Ancestral File* offered by the Church of Jesus Christ of Latter Day Saints in Salt Lake City. *Personal Ancestral File* differs from its competition in several important ways. The first is the low cost of its quite extensive software package, which probably accounts for much of its wide-spread popularity. *PAF* also presents a practical approach to effective family record management; in order to use the program properly, the user must first learn to organize his note-keeping and source documentation to guarantee the benefit of *PAF*'s efficient standard of record searching and retrieval.

But another and more significant function of *Personal Ancestral File* is a phase of one of its three-part programs, a unique medium of exchange standard called GEDCOM, an acronym for Genealogical Data Communications. GEDCOM is a file transfer system that has the ability to convert your family records to a transmission data format that adapts the records to work on another *PAF* or similar program. Reversely, records received from a *Personal Ancestral File* or similar program can be converted by GEDCOM back to the required format for use on a receiving computer. This unique function of GEDCOM will allow genealogists around the world to exchange family information with one another without having to re-enter all the data thereby enabling them to easily share genealogical and historical data.

The Genealogical Library of the Church of the Latter Day Saints is at present computerizing its huge microfilmed collection of ancestral data, a prodigious undertaking. To date, the family records that have been computerized so far are accessible only in person at the LDS Church in Salt Lake City. It is hoped that in the near future, with the assistance of GEDCOM, the Church can offer a comprehensive central database that will afford computer access to all of the family records in its Genealogical Library. When this happens, perhaps there will be a true family-of-man hook-up that links all of our records together into one vast database of ancestral information. But, as yet, this is still down the road.

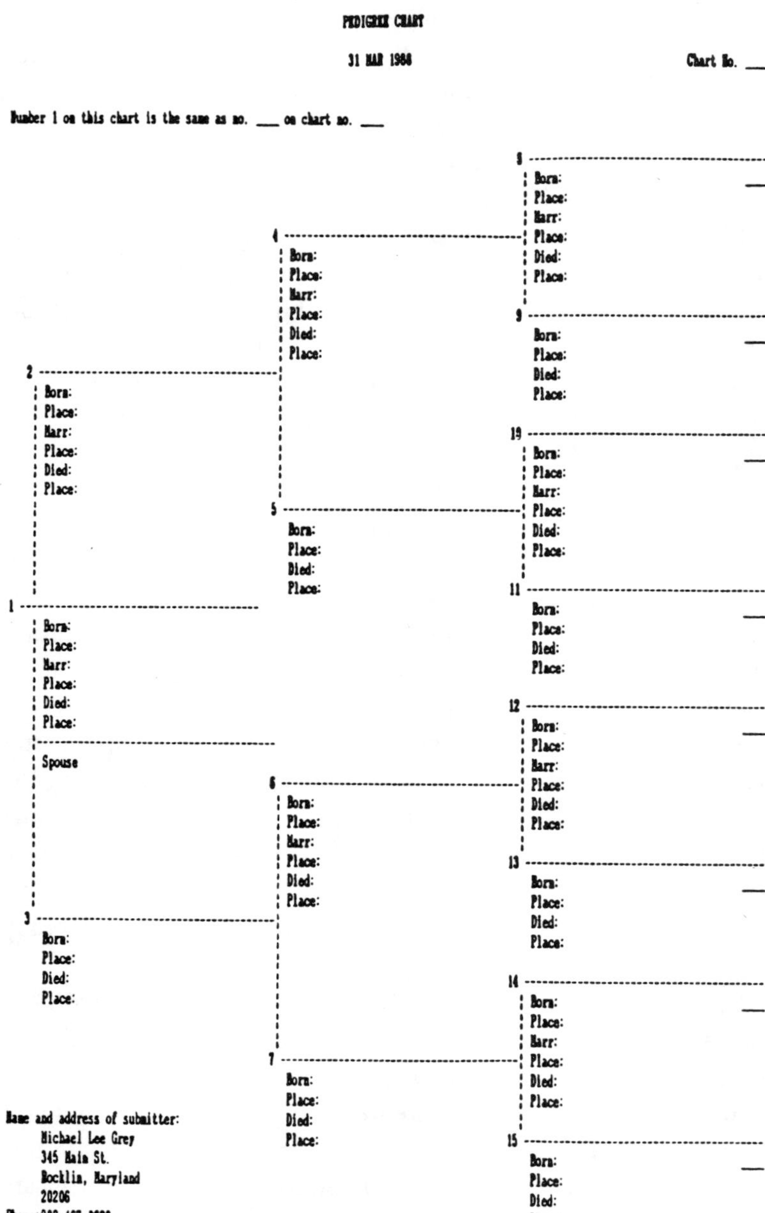

PEDIGREE CHART

31 MAR 1988

Chart No. ___

Number 1 on this chart is the same as no. ___ on chart no. ___

8
Born:
Place:
Marr:
Place:
Died:
Place:

4
Born:
Place:
Marr:
Place:
Died:
Place:

9
Born:
Place:
Died:
Place:

2
Born:
Place:
Marr:
Place:
Died:
Place:

10
Born:
Place:
Marr:
Place:
Died:
Place:

5
Born:
Place:
Died:
Place:

11
Born:
Place:
Died:
Place:

1
Born:
Place:
Marr:
Place:
Died:
Place:

Spouse

12
Born:
Place:
Marr:
Place:
Died:
Place:

6
Born:
Place:
Marr:
Place:
Died:
Place:

13
Born:
Place:
Died:
Place:

3
Born:
Place:
Died:
Place:

14
Born:
Place:
Marr:
Place:
Died:
Place:

7
Born:
Place:
Died:
Place:

15
Born:
Place:
Died:
Place:

Name and address of submitter:
Michael Lee Grey
345 Main St.
Rocklin, Maryland
20206
Phone: 902-467-0628

Figure 23: Pedigree Chart—Blank

Computer printout of Personal Ancestral File,
courtesy of the Church of Jesus Christ of Latter Day Saints)

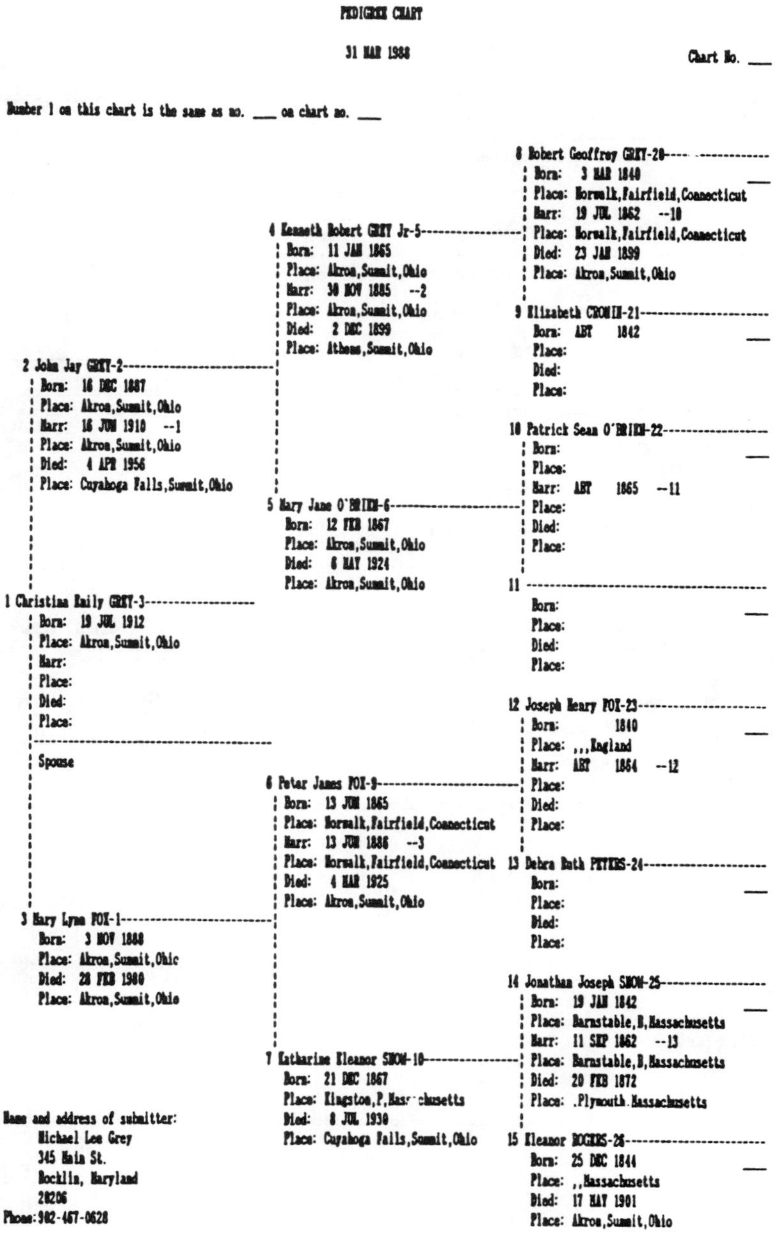

PEDIGREE CHART

31 MAR 1988

Chart No. ___

Number 1 on this chart is the same as no. ___ on chart no. ___

1 Christina Emily GREY-3
Born: 19 JUL 1912
Place: Akron,Summit,Ohio
Marr:
Place:
Died:
Place:

Spouse

2 John Jay GREY-2
Born: 16 DEC 1887
Place: Akron,Summit,Ohio
Marr: 16 JUN 1910 --1
Place: Akron,Summit,Ohio
Died: 4 APR 1956
Place: Cuyahoga Falls,Summit,Ohio

3 Mary Lynn FOX-1
Born: 3 NOV 1888
Place: Akron,Summit,Ohic
Died: 28 FEB 1980
Place: Akron,Summit,Ohio

4 Kenneth Robert GREY Jr-5
Born: 11 JAN 1865
Place: Akron,Summit,Ohio
Marr: 30 NOV 1885 --2
Place: Akron,Summit,Ohio
Died: 2 DEC 1899
Place: Athens,Summit,Ohio

5 Mary Jane O'BRIEN-6
Born: 12 FEB 1867
Place: Akron,Summit,Ohio
Died: 6 MAY 1924
Place: Akron,Summit,Ohio

6 Peter James FOX-9
Born: 13 JUN 1865
Place: Norwalk,Fairfield,Connecticut
Marr: 13 JUN 1886 --3
Place: Norwalk,Fairfield,Connecticut
Died: 4 MAR 1925
Place: Akron,Summit,Ohio

7 Katharine Eleanor SNOW-10
Born: 21 DEC 1867
Place: Kingston,P,Massachusetts
Died: 8 JUL 1930
Place: Cuyahoga Falls,Summit,Ohio

8 Robert Geoffrey GREY-20
Born: 3 MAR 1840
Place: Norwalk,Fairfield,Connecticut
Marr: 19 JUL 1862 --10
Place: Norwalk,Fairfield,Connecticut
Died: 23 JAN 1899
Place: Akron,Summit,Ohio

9 Elizabeth CRONIN-21
Born: ABT 1842
Place:
Died:
Place:

10 Patrick Sean O'BRIEN-22
Born:
Place:
Marr: ABT 1865 --11
Place:
Died:
Place:

11
Born:
Place:
Died:
Place:

12 Joseph Henry FOX-23
Born: 1840
Place: ,,,England
Marr: ABT 1864 --12
Place:
Died:
Place:

13 Debra Ruth PETERS-24
Born:
Place:
Died:
Place:

14 Jonathan Joseph SNOW-25
Born: 19 JAN 1842
Place: Barnstable,B,Massachusetts
Marr: 11 SEP 1862 --13
Place: Barnstable,B,Massachusetts
Died: 20 FEB 1872
Place: .Plymouth Massachusetts

15 Eleanor ROGERS-26
Born: 25 DEC 1844
Place: ,,Massachusetts
Died: 17 MAY 1901
Place: Akron,Summit,Ohio

Name and address of submitter:
Michael Lee Grey
345 Main St.
Rocklin, Maryland
20206
Phone:302-467-0628

Figure 24: Pedigree Chart—Completed
(Computer printout of Personal Ancestral File, courtesy of the Church of Jesus Christ of Latter Day Saints)

```
==============================================================================
MARRIAGE ENTRY  (for sealing wife to husband)
==============================================================================
Name and address of submitter:

                                                 Stake Number:
                                                Stake/Mission:
                                                   Home Phone:
------------------------------------------------------------------------------
For the couple submitted on this form, mark the box for one of the following
options:
[ ] Option 1--TEMPLE FILE  Send all names to any temple and assign proxies
                           for sealing.
[ ] Option 2--FAMILY FILE  Send all names to my family file at the __________
                           Temple.  I will provide proxies for sealing.
==============================================================================
==============================================================================
MARRIAGE DATA
    MARRIAGE PLACE:
    MARRIAGE  DATE:
------------------------------------------------------------------------------
HUSBAND
       GIVEN NAMES:
           SURNAME:                DEATH DATE:                  MARR. AGE:
------------------------------------------------------------------------------
WIFE
       GIVEN NAMES:
           SURNAME:                DEATH DATE:                  MARR. AGE:
==============================================================================
HUSBAND'S PARENTS
    Father
       GIVEN NAMES:
           SURNAME:
    Mother
       GIVEN NAMES:
           SURNAME:
==============================================================================
WIFE'S PARENTS
    Father
       GIVEN NAMES:
           SURNAME:
    Mother
       GIVEN NAMES:
           SURNAME:
==============================================================================
Your relationship to husband/wife:

==============================================================================
DATA SOURCE:


==============================================================================
```

Figure 25: Marriage Entry Form—Blank

(Computer printout of Personal Ancestral File, courtesy of the Church of Jesus Christ of Latter Day Saints)

```
==============================================================================
MARRIAGE ENTRY  (for sealing wife to husband)
==============================================================================
Name and address of submitter:
Michael Lee Grey
345 Main St.                              Stake Number: 1511944
Rocklin, Maryland                        Stake/Mission: Silver Spring Maryland
20206                                       Home Phone: 902-467-0628
------------------------------------------------------------------------------
For the couple submitted on this form, mark the box for one of the following
options:
[ ] Option 1--TEMPLE FILE  Send all names to any temple and assign proxies
                           for sealing.
[ ] Option 2--FAMILY FILE  Send all names to my family file at the __________
                           Temple.  I will provide proxies for sealing.
==============================================================================
==============================================================================
MARRIAGE DATA
    MARRIAGE PLACE: Akron,Summit,Ohio
    MARRIAGE  DATE: 16 JUN 1910
------------------------------------------------------------------------------
HUSBAND
       GIVEN NAMES: John Jay
          SURNAME: Grey              DEATH DATE:  4 APR 1956     MARR. AGE: 23
------------------------------------------------------------------------------
WIFE
       GIVEN NAMES: Mary Lynn
          SURNAME: Fox               DEATH DATE: 28 FEB 1980     MARR. AGE: 22
==============================================================================
HUSBAND'S PARENTS
    Father
       GIVEN NAMES: Kenneth Robert
          SURNAME: Grey
    Mother
       GIVEN NAMES: Mary Jane
          SURNAME: O'Brien
==============================================================================
WIFE'S PARENTS
    Father
       GIVEN NAMES: Peter James
          SURNAME: Fox
    Mother
       GIVEN NAMES: Katharine Eleanor
          SURNAME: Snow
==============================================================================
Your relationship to husband/wife:
                    2ggson
==============================================================================
DATA SOURCE:        Personal records of family members.


==============================================================================
```

Figure 26: Marriage Entry Form—Completed

(Computer printout of Personal Ancestral File, courtesy of the Church of Jesus Christ of Latter Day Saints)

INCOMPLETE INDIVIDUAL ORDINANCES

31 MAR 1988 Page 1

RIN	Name	Br/Ch Year	Death Year	Baptism	Endowment	Seal to Parents
3	Christina Emily GREY	1912				
4	Earl Glen GREY	1914	1982			
5	Kenneth Robert GREY Jr	1865	1899			
6	Mary Jane O'BRIEN	1867	1924			
9	Peter James FOX	1865	1925			
10	Katharine Eleanor SNOW	1867	1930			
11	Joseph Raymond DRAPER	1909	1976			
12	Suzanne ANDRE	1914				
13	Lydia Helene GREEN	1919		6 DEC 1927	29 SEP 1942	
14	George Byron GREEN Ii	1888	1950	13 JAN 1940	30 JUN 1942	
15	Lila MC PHERSON	1890	1971	23 MAY 1944	29 AUG 1945	
16	Etienne Robert ANDRE	1891	1930			
17	Eloise Maude PRESTON	1893	1971			
18	Thomas Joseph DRAPER	1885	1942			
19	Edna Geraldine TAYLOR	1890	1955			
20	Robert Geoffrey GREY	1840	1899			
21	Elizabeth CRONIN	1842				
22	Patrick Sean O'BRIEN					
23	Joseph Henry FOX	1840				
24	Debra Ruth PETERS					
25	Jonathan Joseph SNOW	1842	1872			
26	Eleanor ROGERS	1844	1901			
27	GREY					
28	Mary Lynn FOX	1888	1980	14 AUG 1922		
29	John Jay GREY	1887	1956			

INCOMPLETE MARRIAGE SEALINGS

31 MAR 1988 Page 1

MRIN	Husband Name or *Oldest Child	Wife Name	Marr. Year	Sealing Date
1	John Jay GREY-2	Mary Lynn FOX-1	1910	
2	Kenneth Robert GREY Jr-5	Mary Jane O'BRIEN-6	1885	
3	Peter James FOX-9	Katharine E SNOW-10	1886	
4	Joseph R DRAPER-11		1935	
5	Earl Glen GREY-4	Suzanne ANDRE-12	1936	
8	Etienne Robert ANDRE-16	Eloise Maude PRESTON-17	1915	
9	Thomas Joseph DRAPER-18	Edna G TAYLOR-19	1910	
10	Robert Geoffrey GREY-20	Elizabeth CRONIN-21	1862	
11	Patrick Sean O'BRIEN-22		1865	
12	Joseph Henry FOX-23	Debra Ruth PETERS-24	1864	
13	Jonathan Joseph SNOW-25	Eleanor ROGERS-26	1862	
14	John Jay GREY-2	Mary Lynn FOX-1	1910	

Figure 27: Incomplete Individual Ordinances List and Incomplete Marriage Sealings List

(Computer printout of Personal Ancestral File, courtesy of the Church of Jesus Christ of Latter Day Saints)

Notwithstanding *Personal Ancestral File*'s many excellent contributions to genealogical computing, there are a few drawbacks to the LDS Church's genealogy software. For one, its computer selections are rather limited and certain programs are, at times, unexpectedly discontinued. Also, as *PAF*'s software is an extensive three-part package that requires a fairly big memory system, your machine may not be adaptive to the capacity demands of the program so be sure to verify it before you order. To check out the availability and the system requirements of *Personal Ancestral File,* write to: Ancestral File Operations Unit, Genealogical Department, 50 East North Temple Street, Salt Lake City, Utah 84150.

The computer printouts on the previous pages are sample forms from *Personal Ancestral File.* The first two shown are a blank pedigree form (Figure 23) and a filled-out one (Figure 24). The next two are a blank (Figure 25) and a completed marriage entry form (Figure 26). The following index, an incomplete individual ordinance list (Figure 27), is one useful to LDS members. *PAF* offers many other forms including some designed especially for LDS Church members such as the incomplete marriage sealings list (Figure 27).

You are probably wondering at this point which genealogy program would be the ideal one for you. Your answer will depend upon several factors. The first is, do you already have a computer and is it the one you will be using? If so, then you are confined to the genealogy programs that will run on your machine's disk operating system. If you have an earlier model or a limited market computer system, you are probably better off to first ascertain what software choices are available to you. Fortunately they are much easier to find than once as there are many excellent genealogy programs available today.

Matching a genealogy program to your computer, however, will still take a little doing, for there are many points to consider. Will it run on your machine's disk operating system? If so, does the software of your choice require more memory than your computer possesses? If the answer is "yes," you will need to check to see if your machine's RAM can be expanded appropriately. Or, reversely, is the program too limited for your more extensive data collection? Keep in mind that in the future, you will probably be adding to your ancestral records, so try not to restrict yourself to a file size limit. There could be, of course, other factors or functions you may also want to obtain from your software depending upon your individual genealogical needs.

The ideal situation is if you can purchase a computer system specifically for your genealogical collection. Then you can check out all of the existing genealogy software ahead of time and when you find the one that seems tailor-made for you, purchase the hardware that utilizes the program. This is not recommended if your computer is intended for additional uses as it may not be as effective for non-genealogical purposes.

But whether you already have your computer or are contemplating the purchase, you need to know of the availability of certain genealogy software and there are several sources to check. For instance, the publication *The Genealogical Helper,* The Everton Publishers, Inc., P.O. Box 368, Logan, Utah 84321, has a special section devoted to computerized genealogy. In these pages can be found advertisements for a number of genealogy software distributors and services. This software ranges from simplistic, inexpensive programs intended for limited memory computers to more extensive and expensive programs designed for big memory computer systems.

If you are unsure as to which software would fill your needs, your best action would be to contact the various software sources directly requesting brochures and computer sample printouts. Some companies also offer an inexpensive demonstration disk to try on your machine with money to be applied to your later purchase.

There are several computer genealogy books available that offer useful instructions, advice, and source material information for anyone interested in this new and challenging pursuit. They include: *Tracing Your Roots by Computer* by Joanna W. Posey, Posey International, P.O. Box 338, Orem, Utah 84057, and *Computer Genealogy* by Paul A. Andereck and Richard A. Pence, Ancestry Inc., P.O. Box 476, Salt Lake City, Utah 84110.

For other computer genealogy sources, the following publications or clubs offer news of the latest developments in the field, plus membership if desired in a computer interest group. Write to:

Genealogical Computing, Ancestry Inc.
P.O Box 476, Salt Lake City, Utah 84110.

The Genealogical Computer Pioneer, Posey International P.O. Box 338, Orem, Utah 84057.

Micro-Roots, 7411 Riggs Road, Adelphi, Maryland 20783.

The National Geographical Society's Interest Group c/o William Johnson, 7304 Mariposa Manassas, Virginia 22711.

The National Society of Computer/Genealogists 1512 Womack, Atlanta, Georgia 30338.

Regarding area computer interest groups, occasionally your local genealogy associations are either affiliated with or have a schedule of the computer genealogy clubs in the vicinity. A check with a nearby library, either regular or genealogical, can usually inform you of the whereabouts and activities of these genealogical associations.

Glossary of Computer Terms

ASCII: American Standard Code For Information Interchange: An electronic code used by most computers to represent information, rather like the dots and dashes of Morse Code. For example, the capital letter "A" is 010001 in ASCII.

BIT: Binary digit: The smallest unit of information in a computer, represented by the on or off state of an electronic circuit. The on/off states are called "one" and "zero."

BYTE: A grouping of eight bits: This is usually the quantity of information that a computer operates on at one time. A byte can represent just about any kind of information, depending on how it is used: a single letter, number, or punctuation mark, part of a number, or part of an instruction in a program telling the computer what to do next.

CD-ROM: Compact Disk Read-Only Memory: A compact laser disk, a reference source purchased with up to 550,000,000 bytes of information already on it.

CPU: Central Processing Unit: An electronic circuit inside the computer that carries out the instructions contained in the package.

CURSOR: A little marker on the display screen that shows you where the next thing you type will go.

DISK DRIVE: A machine into which you insert a floppy disk. The drive rotates the disk and contains a movable magnetic recording head to access the various parts of the disk.

DISPLAY SCREEN: TV-like screen where the computer displays words and/or pictures.

DOT MATRIX: A printer that forms the characters by making little dots on a page.

FILE OR DATABASE MANAGER: A program that lets you computerize collections of data that have been entered in a certain format. You design a "form" to fill out and then use that same form repeatedly to create files.

FLOPPY DISK: A device for storing information permanently. A floppy disk is a flexible disk that can be magnetized to store information. It can be removed from the computer and replaced with another disk much like changing a phonograph record on a turntable.

HARD DISK: Another information storage device. A hard disk differs from a floppy disk in that it can store much more information, it has a much faster response time than a floppy disk and it is usually not removable from the machine.

HARDWARE: Computer equipment.

KEYBOARD: A typewriter-like arrangement of keys used for entering information and commands into the computer.

LASER DISK PLAYER: A device used to run the CD-ROMs. A laser disk player, (or reader) similar to a disk drive is the device required to access the CD-ROM disk.

LETTER QUALITY: A printer that prints with a quality that resembles typeset text.

MODEM: Modulator/Demodulator: A device that permits computers to communicate with other computers over telephone lines.

OPERATING SYSTEMS: A collection of programs that are essential to running a computer system.

PRINTER: A device for putting information from a computer onto paper, rather like a typewriter without a keyboard. Some modern typewriters are computer compatible.

PROGRAM: A set of electronically coded instructions that tells a computer how to perform a task.

RAM: Random Access Memory: The memory circuits that hold the program that the computer is working with. The more RAM you have in your computer, the bigger the programs that you can run in it. The amount of RAM is measured in kilobytes, or "K," which is equal to 1024 bytes. A computer with 64K of RAM has 65,536 bytes of memory, and its capacity is reused many times over while you use the computer, and it is lost when you turn the computer off.

ROM: Read-Only Memory: The computer's built-in memory system which holds a computer's instructions to the user. It cannot be altered, added to, deleted from, or lost from the computer's memory.

SOFTWARE: Computer programs and their instruction manuals.

UTILITY PROGRAMS: Programs that are used for "housekeeping" purposes in a computer system, such as to help you organize your files, get rid of old files you don't need any more, copy files from one disk to another, etc.

WORD PROCESSING: Using a computer to assist in writing letters, books and other documents. Word processing software helps you create, revise and print out documents.

Part Two
IMMIGRATION AND ETHNIC RESEARCH

CHAPTER 13

Immigration History and Research

> Send these, the homeless, tempest-toss'd to me, I
> lift my lamp beside the golden door.
>
> —EMMA LAZARUS

America has been poetically compared to a huge melting pot, a sort of giant crucible wherein all of its immigrant races are continuously blended together to produce a single ethnic group known to the rest of the world as "Americans." Whether or not this so-called merging process is an actuality, or even desirable, is a moot point. A sentiment that seems to be more prevalent today is that immigrants should glory in their folkways and heritages and rejoice in the way that their own culture can enrich the American scene.

However one feels about the "melting pot" metaphor as it pertains to one's own background, there is evidence of the impact that these various foreign cultures have made on the American of today. As an example, where but in the United States do we find such "American" dishes as pizza, goulash, chili, frankfurters, and spaghetti, to name a few? Many of our institutions and customs also arrived with visitors from other lands. Our Christmas tree originated in Germany as did kindergarten, and our Santa Claus was once an honored saint of the New York Dutch. We enjoy smorgasbord restaurants with all of their delicacies, a custom borrowed from the Swedish, as is the log cabin, and St. Patrick's Day has probably never been so enthusiastically celebrated in Ireland as it is here in the United States.

But while we are Americans first, most of us are very aware that we are all the descendants of immigrant forebears, unless, of course, we can claim to be the progeny of the earliest immigrant of them all, the American Indian. This seems to explain a rather curious paradox of the American psyche; although we are proud to be Americans, most of us still harbor a lively curiosity about and experience a certain ethnic pride toward the country or countries that produced our original immigrant progenitors.

But while our curiosity about the backgrounds of our earliest American forebears is natural, it can also, at times, lead us to the point of much exasperation. Diligently tracing an ancestor back through all of the known genealogical sources here in the United States only to find yourself stopped short by a notation, born in "Ireland" or "Germany," without an indication of town or village of birth can be a source of much frustration.

For it is a sad fact that without a beginning point of reference for your overseas search, you will be unable to proceed much further. Knowing the village or at least the area of the country from which the immigrant ancestor originated is pretty much a necessity if the intrepid researcher is to successfully continue his investigation in that country, especially if the ancestor had a particularly common surname. If you feel you have reached this point of frustration in your own ancestor search, but still desire to continue with this line, do not be utterly discouraged. There are many avenues of exploration that can be found in this country. It may be of some assistance if you first have a little historical background on the various times and places of arrival of certain immigrant groups to the United States.

In the days preceding the American Revolution, early immigrants to the English-owned colonies were, predictably, predominantly from the British Isles. After 1700, many Germans also began arriving in the American colonies, fleeing, mainly, the oppressions and restrictions they found at that time in their homeland. These English, Irish, Scottish, and Germans made their homes in all of the thirteen colonies as land was quite plentiful and readily available to them in the new country.

The French and French-speaking settlers had been in North America since before 1600, some of them arriving as far back as 100 years before the English-sponsored *Mayflower* landed at Plymouth Harbor in 1620. These French were the fur traders, explorers, planters, and the missionaries who traveled extensively throughout the New World, leaving settlements as far north as Nova Scotia and as far south as Florida. In the 1700s many French Huguenots, after being driven out of Catholic France, settled in the colonies of South Carolina, New York, and Rhode Island.

Up to the time of the Revolutionary War, more than 200,000 Germans had migrated to the American colonies. Some settled in New York, called New Amsterdam by the early Dutch settlers, and others in Pennsylvania where they became known, erroneously, as "Pennsylvania Dutch." Most of these Germans were from the Rhineland and were seeking a new land where they would be free of restriction in their choice of religion. Pennsylvania, under the pacifist William Penn, especially attracted those who had suffered religious persecution and tyranny in their native lands and wanted no further interference from government.

After the settlement of the Revolutionary War in 1781, immigration was greatly encouraged by the fledgling United States. As a new country with thousands of acres of undeveloped and uncultivated land to be settled, the embryo nation greeted new arrivals to its shores with welcoming arms. As a result, in the beginning immigration to the U.S. was nonselective and members of all nationalities were encouraged to make their homes in the young country.

Even so, European migration to the United States in the beginning of the nineteenth century was almost negligible. After 1815, migration from such countries as Ireland, Germany, and England suddenly began to increase, reaching its peak around 1855. Most of those emigrating between 1815-60 were from Northern and Western Europe. Irish, Germans, and the rest of the British Isles made up most of the contingents with the remainder smaller groups from the Scandinavian countries and the Netherlands. It is said that between 1820 and 1860 more than five million people came to America from overseas and quite a few more unrecorded ones walked across the Canadian border.

After 1848, chaotic revolutions, unemployment, and a severe economic depression in Germany brought another wave of

German immigrants to America. These later Germans settled mainly in the Midwest, traveling up the Mississippi River from New Orleans to colonize along major rivers and waterways in such areas as Ohio, Wisconsin, Indiana, Michigan, Iowa, and Missouri. Wisconsin, especially, received a large influx of German immigrants, and by 1850 Milwaukee was predominantly a German town. Other Germans were among the first of the colonizing settlers to enter the Pacific Northwest, establishing German cities in Oregon and in Southern California where they developed the cultivation of oranges, later to become a major crop of the area.

Although most of the Germans and Irish settled in urban centers during this period, other foreign groups, such as the Scandinavians, were attracted to the prairies and timberlands of Wisconsin, Minnesota, and Iowa with terrain so much like the pastoral settings they had known at home. Earlier, Norwegians had crossed the Atlantic on the sloop *Restaurationen*, arriving in western New York in 1825. This vessel has been called the Scandinavian *Mayflower*, and these settlers are considered the forerunners of those who later fled the European upheavals of 1848 to settle in the northern United States around the Great Lakes region and the upper Missouri and Mississippi rivers. Overpopulation in their fishing villages had driven many Norwegians, Swedes, Danes, and Finns to seek a land that offered not only political freedom, but plenty of free land and flowing, abundant streams.

These were not the first Scandinavians in America. An abortive early attempt to settle a colony called New Sweden on the Delaware River in the seventeenth century had met with a disastrous rout at the hands of a Dutch garrison already established in New Amsterdam. This task force, sent by the irascible Dutch governor, Peter Stuyvesant, ran off the Swedish interlopers without firing a shot, and any further early attempts at settlement in the New World by the Swedes were not repeated.

The Civil War temporarily slowed down the flood of immigration, but soon afterwards, a great labor shortage developed in the United States. The vast hordes of immigrants increased even more as the arrival of steam-powered ships and the expansion of the railroad in Europe and the U.S. further facilitated the flight of emigrants from their mother countries.

The growth of industrial United States had created not only a need for manpower for the factories, but also for consumers to buy the goods produced.

American manufacturers soon began sending agents to Europe to conscript skilled workers from the towns of England, Wales, Greece, and Italy. Later, American unions, fighting what they considered a threat to the local workers, discouraged this kind of recruiting by forcing the passage of the Contract Labor Law in 1885. It outlawed the practice of hiring an emigrant prior to his arrival in the United States.

Many forces drove these exiles from their homelands toward the new nation with its enticements of an abundance of food, land, and especially freedom, commodities sorely lacking in the oppressive climate of nineteenth century Europe. The miseries of Europe following the Napoleonic Wars and the offers of free land in the newly acquired territories of the Northwest and Louisiana did much to further lure many new settlers to the rapidly developing America.

Roughly half of these immigrants were driven by starvation from the impoverished land of Ireland, with Irish immigration reaching its peak after the great potato famine of 1846. The majority of the Irish settled in large port cities such as Boston and New York where, by 1855, one-third of the voting population were native-born Irish. Although most were peasant-born, disillusion with farming and greedy landlords turned these Irish immigrants away from the land and toward the construction and domestic work that was readily available to them in the larger cities of the nation.

Around the latter part of the nineteenth century, railroad agents from America began to comb many European towns and villages with offers of free land for emigrants who would settle on and develop the railroad lines. The new states of Minnesota, Nebraska, Kansas, and Wisconsin were among those that also sent agents to Europe with beguiling posters offering free land to entice new settlers. Consequently, many Czechs were lured to the state of Nebraska, and Russian-German Mennonites went to Kansas to settle on their newly acquired homesteads.

During the 1880s in Czarist Russia, a wave of dreaded organized massacres called *pogroms* swept the country. Russian Jews were attacked by mobs of peasants who, egged on by the authorities, burned and destroyed their homes. A number of these

Russian Jews came to America during this period of their first great exodus. Many of them, along with the Jews from Poland, ended up in the sweat shops of the garment trade in New York. Many of the earlier Jews who came to America had become itinerant peddlers and, as such, made out much better, sometimes following the prospectors and settlers who had migrated to the West in an attempt to seek their fortunes. When it came to finding the yellow gold, in most cases the peddlers were the only ones who prospered by selling supplies to the hopeful prospectors.

Immigration after the 1880s brought an increasing number of emigrants from southern and eastern Europe, countries that, up until that time, had contributed little to the immigration stream that flowed into America. But the period from 1890 to 1907 was the era of the greatest immigration of these people with most coming from Greece, Hungary, Italy, Poland, Portugal, Russia, and Spain. The old Austro-Hungarian Empire contributed the Czechs, the Slovaks, the Hungarians, the Serbs, and the Poles.

Some of the earliest Poles in America had been a small group of refugees who came to the New World after an ill-fated Polish revolution in 1830-31, to settle on public lands in Illinois. By 1890 many Poles were residing in cities such as New York and Milwaukee, while others found work in the steel mills and factories of Pittsburgh and Detroit. It has been estimated that more than two million Poles settled in industrial America during this particular period.

Italian migration to the New World had been limited mostly to those who had come from northern Italy in the early nineteenth century. Most of these early immigrants settled in New York or migrated to California where they worked in agriculture and helped to develop the wine industry in that state; later emigrants from Italy came from southern Italy and Sicily, leaving the poor economic conditions and overpopulation that was so prevalent in their homeland. Most of these southern Italians settled in the port cities of the United States where they found work in construction and the building of railroads. Southern Italians built large sections of the New York subway and carried pipe and poured cement in the cities of Baltimore, Buffalo, Pittsburgh, and Providence.

Why were the immigrants willing to work at such heavy labor? The majority of these foreign-born, although having been farmers in the old country, were drawn into industrial American mainly because they were able to go freely to whatever areas offered a guarantee of work and wages. Compared to their previous run-down farms to which most of them were bonded, work in the stockyards and railroads of Chicago, the factories of Detroit, and the garment-making center of New York offered a far more attractive alternative, albeit back-breaking and dangerous, than starving in their native lands.

Back in Europe, a network of railroads came from all over the continent with their cars filled with travelers destined for such ports of embarkation as Liverpool, Le Havre, and Bremen. Emigrants from Russia, Germany, and the vast Austro-Hungarian Empire usually headed for the bustling city of Hamburg. Other ports such as Constantinople, Piraeus, Antwerp, Rotterdam, and Glasgow also handled a large number of emigrants, all headed for their *El Dorado,* that fabulous land of gold-America.

At first most of the newcomers from Europe landed in the seaports between Boston and Baltimore and stayed mostly in that part of the country. However, after 1855, the majority of the European immigrants entered the country through New York City's Castle Garden, located at the tip of Manhattan Island. Soon this old fort and one-time amusement park was too crowded and poorly equipped to handle the multitudes that were pouring into America. Because of this, many immigrants managed to slip past the authorities into their newly adopted country before the adoption was completed, so to speak.

In an effort to correct this situation, a law was passed in 1882 placing control of admitting aliens under the federal government at all ports of entry. By 1891, a tougher immigration law was enacted with the various reasons for the detention and deportation of aliens spelled out. In 1892, another federal receiving station for processing immigrants was opened at Ellis Island located in New York Harbor. This new station was larger and considered more secure since it was reachable only by water.

Not all incoming foreign travelers were required to be processed through Ellis Island; first- and second-class passengers could land immediately, disembarking directly onto Manhattan Island. All steerage passengers, however, were taken by ferry to Ellis Island. Many of the immigrants were detained there for various reasons and for varying periods of time. Some waited to be picked up by family members. Others were there for a review of their cases, and still others were detained as a "public risk" and, as a result, were unfortunate enough to hear that dreaded edict, "deportation!"

Some of the immigrants were never destined to leave Ellis Island. It has been said that more than a few of the deportees disappeared over the side into the black waters of New York Harbor, apparently preferring a watery grave to facing deportation back to the tyranny, oppression, and possible death awaiting them in their motherlands. Ellis Island was, indeed, well-named "Isle of Tears" by so many of the unfortunates who never made it through to America's "Promised Land."

Most Asian immigrants, first from China, and later Japan, entered America on the Pacific coast. Early immigration processing for the Chinese was conducted in a warehouse rented from the Pacific Mail Steamship Company in San Francisco. After 1910, all Asian immigrants to the U.S. were first required to be held in quarantine on Angel Island in San Francisco Bay. This quarantine, which sometimes lasted weeks or even months, was due in part to official fears of epidemics such as cholera thought to be prevalent in the East at that time.

The first Chinese arrived on the West Coast during the 1850s and, in the beginning, were able to eke out a living reworking old abandoned mining claims. Soon, many of them went to work building the Central Pacific Railroad where they were much in demand, sometimes working for as little as two cents a day. After the completion of the railroad, trade unions and white labor groups complained about the importing of such cheap labor. Bowing to these pressure groups, the United States enacted one of the first of its laws designed to change its open door policy when, in 1870, it refused citizenship to the Chinese. In 1882, the Chinese Exclusion Act was passed, which further restricted Chinese immigration. This measure remained in effect until it was rescinded by President Franklin D. Roosevelt in 1943, probably in deference to the United States' World War II ally, Nationalist China.

For most Japanese, migration to the American mainland came later, since emigration from Japan was not even allowed until after 1868, and then without return privileges. Not until 1890 were most Japanese officially allowed by their emperor to leave their homeland. As a result many Japanese came to the United States to escape the oppression and poverty that were rife in their country at that time. Many of them settled in Hawaii or in California where they turned to farming and were quite successful.

In 1907, a pact called the "Gentlemen's Agreement" between Japan and the U.S. provided that no Japanese laborer headed for the United States would receive a passport from the Japanese government. This was apparently in response to threatened legislation by the U.S. that would close the door to Japanese immigration, a policy reflecting the growing fear of the increasing Japanese labor force in the country. Further restrictive legislation against the Japanese was later enacted with the passage of the Japanese Exclusion Act of 1924 that completely closed the door temporarily to Japanese immigration to the United States.

Other restrictive acts toward the Japanese included the detention of even native-born Japanese-Americans in the internment camps in the United States during World War II. This internment of Japanese was due to the war hysteria, especially on the West Coast, resulting from Japan's December 7, 1941, air attack on the American naval base at Pearl Harbor in the Hawaiian Islands, the event which triggered the United States' entry into World War II. In 1952, the McCurran-Walter Act removed all racial bars for entry into the United States and American citizenship could be granted to the Japanese.

Although most immigrants came to America on crowded, ill-equipped passenger ships, there were others who merely crossed the border from either Mexico or Canada, a short trip by land on foot, on horseback, or by carriage.

Among the first Canadians to come to the American colonies were the French-Canadians from Nova Scotia who had been evicted from Canada by the British in 1775. From Acadia, they settled mostly in Louisiana where their descendants later became known as "Cajuns." In the latter part of the nineteenth century, a large number of French-Canadians crossed the U.S. border to settle in the New England states of Maine and Vermont where they found work in the textile mills.

Because of the easy entry into the United States from Canada, a large number of such immigrants have gone unrecorded. Many emigrants from Scotland settled in Ontario, Canada, in the nineteenth century and later entered the United States. From 1815-60 alone, at least 112,000 known entrants from Canada and Newfoundland, many of whom were undoubtedly European-born, crossed the U.S. border.

Emigration in the past from our southern neighbor, Mexico, also has been especially heavy. Spanish-speaking immigrants today comprise one of the largest ethnic groups in America. Most of the Hispanic-Americans are descended from Spanish or Mexican ancestors who lived in such areas of the Southwest as California, New Mexico, Arizona, and Texas when these territories were still part of Mexico. After the settlement of the Mexican War in 1848, these people automatically became citizens of the United States under the Treaty of Guadulupe Hidalgo and were permitted to keep their estates and previously-owned land holdings in their new country.

From the beginning of the United States to the twentieth century, emigration from Mexico was freely allowed and many Spanish-speaking people entered the nation during this period. Those who came by boat did so usually through Galveston, New Orleans, or San Diego, while those who came by land usually crossed the border by way of Texas, New Mexico, Arizona, or California. After 1903, when Mexican emigration began to be restricted, and up until 1952, the only point of legal entry into the U.S. was El Paso, Texas. Since that time, emigrants from Mexico have been permitted to enter the United States through any port of entry.

The largest influx of Spanish-speaking people to the U.S. has occurred since 1920 with immigrants coming from Mexico, the West Indies, South and Central America, Cuba, and the Philippines. There are also a large number of Puerto Ricans who have not been recorded, because they are considered American citizens, Puerto Rico having been a U.S. territory since 1917. Many of the early Puerto Ricans who came to the United States settled in an area of New York City known as Spanish Harlem. It has been claimed that in 1970 there were more Puerto Ricans in New York than there were in San Juan, Puerto Rico.

Today all racial barriers to the United States have been lifted and the only quota remaining has to do with immigration from the Western Hemisphere as compared with that of the Eastern

Hemisphere. Even this is not entirely restrictive; the quota from individual countries can be adjusted accordingly, depending upon the immigration pool to which the entire world contributes. This policy is considered much more objective and humane toward those who enter America these days than the discriminatory and arbitrary procedures that dictated the naturalization practices of this country in its not always so glorious past.

Ellis Island was closed down as a receiving center in 1965 and, at present, is part of the Statue of Liberty National Monument. Today's immigrants are screened at all of the different ports of entry into America. If they travel by ship, they are processed on board before they disembark. If they arrive by plane, they are taken to a special office in the airport for immigration screening. The whole processing usually takes only a few hours at most. This is a far cry from the dreary weeks of anxious and apprehensive waiting that so characterized the procedures for earlier immigrants, those "huddled masses," who so desperately sought entrance into this country through Emma Lazarus' "golden door."

Why did so many seek entry into this new country of America? There were probably as many reasons as there were people, but they all seemed to have one thing in common; they all desired to make their home in this land. Immigration was not confined to the poor. Men and women of wealth, science, and the arts were also among those who joined the mainstream of immigrant travel to America for reasons that ranged from economic and religious to that of self-preservation.

Americans have been described by some historians as "the choosing people," based upon the fact that, for the most part, they or their forebears initially chose to make the arduous and sometimes difficult journey to America. With the exception of the unfortunate, abducted blacks, most newcomers to America have been willing, and for the most part, anxious to seek out whatever the new land had to offer.

Ascertaining not only when your own particular ancestor elected to make his odyssey to this country, but from what point of origin, can be one of the most rewarding and stimulating, if somewhat painstaking enterprises, a diligent ancestor hunter can undertake. It is also a necessary one. Unless you have information on the town or village of your forebear's origin and his date of migration, you will probably find your out-of-country search immediately stymied. If you have searched all of your ancestor's personal and vital records without uncovering his last legal residence or place of birth, then it is time to turn to certain official records available in this country. Among the most useful research sources are the immigration records including ships' passenger lists and naturalization records.

Passenger arrival records, especially, can provide much valuable genealogical information. These lists, maintained by the captains and the masters of the ships as well as by the immigration officials at the port of entry, contain such data as the name of the vessel, the passenger's name, age, and sex, date, and port of arrival, his destination in the United States, and his point of origin in the old country. Some records also indicated if the passenger died en route with documentation of the date and circumstance of his death.

One must be forewarned, however, that there are some drawbacks in the use of passenger arrival records. They are, unfortunately, sometimes limited in scope, occasionally giving only the country of origin and not the town or village. Other records are missing or extremely illegible and difficult to read. A further disability in researching passenger lists is that there are so many of them. Only certain ones have been indexed and alphabetized, which means that to avoid a consummate amount of searching, one would need to know the port of entry, the name of the vessel, and the approximate date of arrival. In addition to these drawbacks, there are also restrictions on certain passenger arrival records; the lists and their indexes are considered confidential and access to National Archives passenger lists is limited to those that are over fifty years old.

In spite of all these shortcomings, passenger ship records can still hold a wealth of genealogical information if you locate the appropriate ones. They can pinpoint a time of arrival and a destination for the ancestor. They can, at times, indicate a place and date of birth for the passenger, while giving, also, the names of other family members, either on board or at the destination in the United States. In addition, some of the records give the port the passenger sailed from as well as his occupation.

Two types of passenger lists can be found in the National Archives: Custom Passenger Lists and Immigration Passenger Lists.

Custom passenger lists, established by an act of 1819, required the master of each ship entering an American port from a foreign one to file a list of its passengers with the district collector of customs, hence the name. These passenger lists include such information as the name of the vessel, the date of its arrival, the port of embarkation, and the name, age, sex, occupation, and country of origin for each passenger. The National Archives has original custom passenger lists dating from 1820 to 1902 and copies and abstracts of lists from 1820 to 1905.

The New Colossus.

Not like the brazen giant of Greek fame,
With conquering limbs astride from land to land;
Here at our sea-washed, sunset-gates shall stand
A mighty woman with a torch, whose flame
Is the imprisoned lightning, and her name
Mother of Exiles. From her beacon-hand
Glows world-wide welcome, her mild eyes command
The air-bridged harbor ~~that~~ twin-cities frame.

"Keep, ancient lands, your storied pomp!" cries she,
With silent lips. "Give me your tired, your poor,
Your huddled masses yearning to breathe free,
The wretched refuse of your teeming shore,–
Send these, the homeless, tempest-tost to me,
I lift my lamp beside the golden door!"

Emma Lazarus.

November 2nd 1883.

Figure 28: "The New Colossus" by Emma Lazarus
(facsimile)

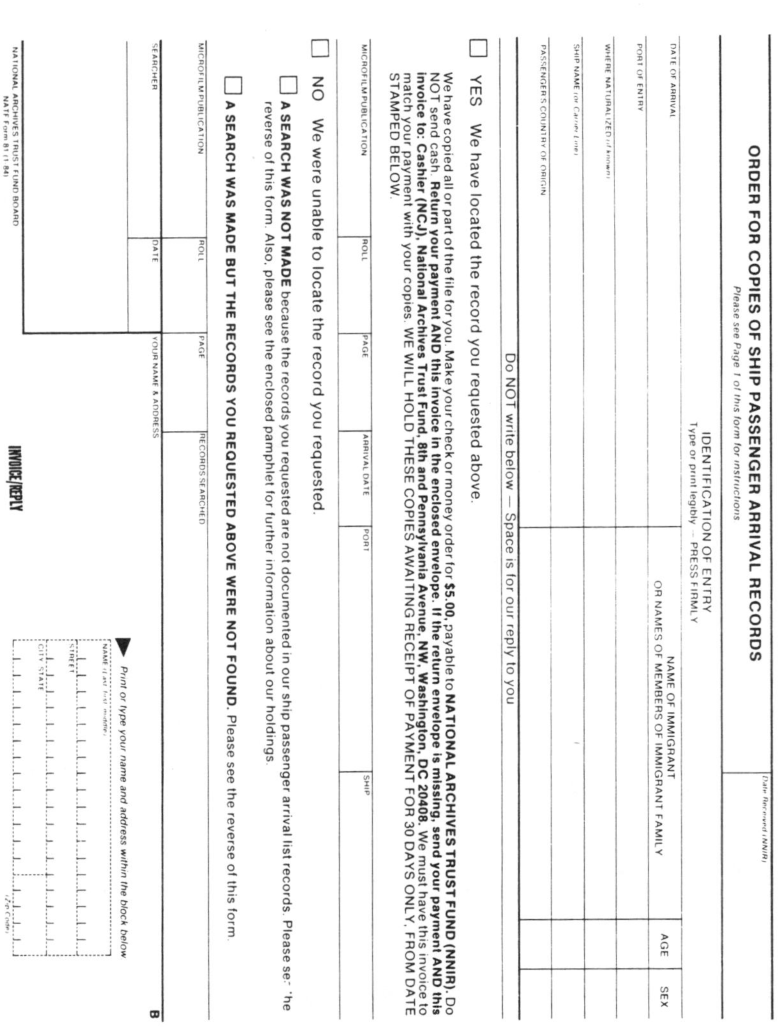

ORDER FOR COPIES OF SHIP PASSENGER ARRIVAL RECORDS

Please see Page 1 of this form for instructions

Date Received (NNIR)

IDENTIFICATION OF ENTRY
Type or print legibly — PRESS FIRMLY

	NAME OF IMMIGRANT OR NAMES OF MEMBERS OF IMMIGRANT FAMILY	AGE	SEX
DATE OF ARRIVAL			
PORT OF ENTRY			
WHERE NATURALIZED (if known)			
SHIP NAME (or Carrier Line)			
PASSENGER'S COUNTRY OF ORIGIN			

Do NOT write below — Space is for our reply to you

☐ YES We have located the record you requested above.

We have copied all or part of the file for you. Make your check or money order for **$5.00**, payable to **NATIONAL ARCHIVES TRUST FUND (NNIR)**. Do NOT send cash. **Return your payment AND this invoice in the enclosed envelope. If the return envelope is missing, send your payment AND this invoice to: Cashier (NCJ), National Archives Trust Fund, 8th and Pennsylvania Avenue, NW, Washington, DC 20408.** We must have this invoice to match your payment with your copies. WE WILL HOLD THESE COPIES AWAITING RECEIPT OF PAYMENT FOR 30 DAYS ONLY, FROM DATE STAMPED BELOW.

MICROFILM PUBLICATION	ROLL	PAGE	ARRIVAL DATE	PORT	SHIP

☐ NO We were unable to locate the record you requested.

☐ **A SEARCH WAS NOT MADE** because the records you requested are not documented in our ship passenger arrival list records. Please see the reverse of this form. Also, please see the enclosed pamphlet for further information about our holdings.

☐ **A SEARCH WAS MADE BUT THE RECORDS YOU REQUESTED ABOVE WERE NOT FOUND.** Please see the reverse of this form.

MICROFILM PUBLICATION	ROLL	PAGE	RECORDS SEARCHED

SEARCHER	DATE	YOUR NAME & ADDRESS

▶ *Print or type your name and address within the block below*

NAME (Last, first, middle)
STREET
CITY STATE ZIP Code

B

NATIONAL ARCHIVES TRUST FUND BOARD
NATF Form 81 (1-84)

INVOICE/REPLY

Figure 29: Order for Copies of Ship Passenger Arrival Records
(Courtesy of the National Archives, Washington, D.C.)

The main advantage of the custom passenger lists is the fact that they were alphabetized and indexed by the Works Progress Administration in the 1930s. This makes them easier to research than the unindexed immigration passenger lists. However, even though your forebear's records may be easier to locate in the alphabetized index, the data may not be as complete, since some of them do not indicate the town or village of origin for the ancestor, information vital for overseas research.

Immigration passenger lists were established by a federal act of 1882. Those found in the National Archives cover the period 1883 through 1945. Immigration passenger lists generally reveal the name and the master of the vessel, the passenger's name, age, and sex, his occupation, place and date of birth, and his last legal residence. After 1893, further information about the immigrant was added including his destination in the United States, the names of family members located there, and their relationship to him. This later data makes the immigration passenger lists invaluable for foreign research.

Unfortunately, immigration passenger lists, too, have their drawbacks. They were never indexed or alphabetized and are listed first by port and then chronologically by date of arrival. One would have to know the port, the date of arrival, and the name of the vessel in order to research the records for a particular ancestor. Also, both immigration and custom passenger lists contained the names of not only immigrants, but of visitors and returning U.S. citizens who had been abroad.

Most of the passenger lists in the National Archives are on microfilm that are available for review. If you know the specific date of arrival or the ship's name, it is possible to obtain by mail a copy of the passenger arrival record from the archives. To obtain information on how to order copies of the records, send a request for NAFT Form 40(12-79), Order and Billing for Copies of Passenger Arrival Records, to Reference Services Branch (NNIR), General Services Administration, Washington, D.C. 20408.

For further information the publication, *Genealogical Research in the National Archives,* has a chapter on the passenger lists that are available for public review in the archives. This volume also offers other reading suggestions on material not contained in the National Archives such as a multi-volumed series called *Ship and*

Rail, compiled by San Francisco historian, Louis Rasmussen, and published by San Francisco Historical Records, 1204 Nimitz Drive, Colma, CA 94015. It tells of some ship passenger arrivals to the West Coast from 1850 through 1975. Also included is a compilation of data on the migrants who came to San Francisco by railroad from 1870 to 1890.

During the nineteenth century, most foreign visitors to America entered the country through the very active port of New York. A valuable source of information on some of those people is the excellent publication, *The Morton Allan Directory of European Passenger Steamship Arrivals*, put out by Immigrant Information, Inc., New York. This directory, located in many libraries, lists the names and dates of arrival for steamships that entered the port of New York from 1890 through 1930. Data found in this publication can be especially useful if you do not know your forebear's approximate date or port of arrival, but do know the name of the vessel. Once you find out the date of the ship's arrival from the directory, you can send to the National Archives for any passenger arrival information they may have on your ancestor.

Although the National Archives records are limited to ninety-five Atlantic and Gulf of Mexico ports, there are a number of other sources where passenger lists for other ports can be located. Most of these lists have been privately published for research purposes and can usually be located in most genealogical libraries and many historical societies. The Church of Jesus Christ of the Latter Day Saints in Salt Lake City also has an extensive collection of passenger arrival records including some of the original lists transferred from the National Archives.

Although many of the early colonial passenger lists have been lost, the information in them has survived to a certain degree. One extremely comprehensive collection of data on early passenger arrival records is a multi-volumed set called *A Bibliography of Ships Passenger Lists, 1539-1825*, originally compiled by Harold Lancour, but updated as *Passenger Lists Bibliography*, edited by P. William Filby. This collection of books is a bibliography of passenger lists that covers the colonial period of the United States up through the nineteenth century. It includes the passenger's name, age, place and year of arrival, accompanying passengers and a code indicating from what source the original passenger list information was taken.

Any data found in this publication can be extremely valuable to the genealogical researcher even if the original source of information may no longer be available. If one can determine an approximate arrival date for the immigrant, it may be possible to use the information to uncover other pertinent facts on the ancestor in question. If, for example, you have received sufficient information from the passenger lists, you may have enough data to contact the Immigration and Naturalization Service for a copy of your forebear's naturalization petition. This subject will be discussed a little later in this chapter.

On occasion one can find a collection of passenger lists that affords not only information on a particular ancestor, but also a glimpse into the past at some of the conditions surrounding early American immigration. An intriguing early book of passenger arrival records is entitled *The Original List of Persons of Quality,* and subtitled rather tellingly, *Emigrants; Religious Exiles; Political Rebels, Serving Men Sold For A Period of Years; Apprentices; Children Stolen, Maidens Pressed; and Others Who Went From Great Britain to the American Plantations 1600-1700.* This publication, edited by John Camden Hotten and first published in 1874, includes passenger lists for such vessels as the first colonial ship to New England, the *Mayflower,* as well as the one to follow, the *Fortune.*

Also included in this small volume are some historical notes taken from Governor William Bradford's *History of the Plymouth Colony* in which he refers to a passenger, one John Alden, as a "hopeful young man," further mentioning that "he later married Pricilla Mullen . . . and had eleven children." Governor Bradford also mentions, rather dispassionately, that of the one hundred "souls" who first arrived on the *Mayflower* in 1620, over one-half of them died within a few months of reaching Plymouth Rock.

Notwithstanding the high mortality rates and the miserable first years that so often characterized the lot of many of this country's original colonists, they still came, doggedly chopping their way through the wilderness to clear out small patches of land they could claim as their own. Most of these settlers were from countries controlled by the British Crown, and as such, automatic citizenship was conferred upon them in the then British-owned America colonies. However, after the American Revolution, steps were taken by the young country to initiate a more official naturalization process for the many foreigners who were soon to flock to America's shores.

Naturalization in the United States is the process by which an alien becomes a citizen and lives in this country with almost all of the rights and privileges of one who is native born. The first naturalization law in the U.S., enacted in 1790, provided that an unbonded white male could petition for citizenship by applying to any common law court of record in any state in which he had resided for at least one year. He also had to reside in the country two years before he could apply, a term that was increased to five years in 1795 and that still prevails today.

At first, naturalization was conferred by the individual states, but after the passage of the Fourteenth Amendment in 1858, the acquisition of U.S. citizenship became a national right to be granted only by the federal government. This amendment guaranteed national citizenship to all persons, regardless of sex or race, born or naturalized in the U.S., and subject to its jurisdiction with some exceptions, the most notable being the native-born American Indian.

In 1906, Congress established the Bureau of Immigration and Naturalization, an agency charged with the expedition of specific standards to be adopted by it and those courts qualified to handle naturalization proceedings. Before, only the courts handled all naturalization matters, so prior to 1906, such records are found in the custody of the particular court of jurisdiction, whether city, county, state, or federal. As of September 27, 1906, the Immigration and Naturalization Service, as it is now known, has acquired duplicate copies of all naturalization records issued from that time on.

Federal naturalization records usually comprise a number of things including a declaration of intention (no longer required), the petition for naturalization, the witnesses' depositions regarding the petitioner's character, the record of the final oath of allegiance, and the court order admitting the petitioner to citizenship. Sometimes an ancestor hunter is lucky enough to find a complete packet among the archives records called "petition and record" that includes all of these documents. This is a great boon to the researcher as just about all of the records vital to an overseas investigation can be found here in one fell swoop.

One can ascertain, as a general rule, from these records, the immigrant's date and place of birth, occupation, date of arrival in the U.S., the name of the ship, and the port of arrival. After 1906, even more important information was required from the immigrant; his personal description, present address as well as his foreign one, the names of his parents, and the dates and places of birth and residences of all his children.

Naturalization records can be found in many sources. As indicated before, prior to 1906, all of the naturalization records are located only in the actual courts that performed the naturalization procedures. To find out where your ancestor's records are, you should attempt to contact the appropriate court of processing to see if the documents are still there. If, by some chance, they are, see if you can make arrangements through the clerk of the court to obtain copies of them. If the records have been transferred to an archives, try to obtain from the file, either the number from the declaration of intent or from the petition for naturalization since you will need at least one of these numbers to research most sources.

If you have a problem determining in which court your ancestor's records are located, you may have to conduct a rather painstaking search. Today most naturalization proceedings take place in the federal courts while the bulk of the rest traditionally take place in the state courts. During the nineteenth century, however, all courts were authorized to conduct naturalization proceedings, so the processing could have occurred in any city, county, state, or federal court. In searching for the appropriate court of record for your ancestor, start with whatever court was the most convenient to his place of residence when he filed his declaration of intent. Be aware, however, that the petition for naturalization was usually filed from three to five years later, so it is possible that both his residence and court of record may have changed in the interim, necessitating further research.

To check on a naturalization issued after September 26, 1906, direct your inquiries to the Immigration and Naturalization Service, 425 Eye Street, N.W., Washington, D.C. 20536. A staff member will let you know if the information you seek is available for public review or if it is considered confidential. If the information is accessible, you can send for it on Form N-585, obtainable from any INS district office, and you will receive whatever information they have on your forebear's citizenship records.

The publication *Genealogical Research in the National Archives* has a chapter on naturalization records and where they can be located in the archives. The book also tells how to obtain certain records that are not in the custody of the National Archives. The individual archives branches also have information on the naturalization material that can be found, not only in that particular branch, but in all the other locations. To obtain this information, stop by your nearest archives branch or write to Chief, Archive Branch, Federal Archives and Record Center, at one of the addresses listed at the back of this book.

Once you have diligently researched all of the available local records and have established a specific overseas ancestral point of origin and an approximate date of migration, you are probably wondering, "Where do I go from here?" Knowing these facts may open some doors for you in this country even before you venture to do your overseas searching.

You may find much of the information you need at the Genealogical Library of the Church of Jesus Christ of Latter Day Saints in Salt Lake City, which has one of the most extensive collections of genealogical material in the world. Also known as the LDS or the Mormon Church, this organization has a vast underground storehouse in the Rocky Mountains near Salt Lake City that houses a mammoth collection of genealogical data including all of the U.S. census records, family histories, land grants, marriage records, wills and court records, naturalization records, passenger lists, church and Bible records, and many other documents devoted not only to the U.S., but to countries around the world and to special ethnic groups.

If you can, you should plan a visit in person and check out the extensive microfilm collection. You can do your own search or, for a fee, have the staff do it for a particular ancestor through their "pedigree research service." If you are unable to visit the LDS Genealogical Library in person, you can request a list of the services they provide by writing to Genealogical Society Library, 50 East North Temple Street, Salt Lake City, Utah 84150.

After you have obtained all of the information you can from the LDS collection, it is time to start your overseas investigation.

Foreign research is done pretty much like it is here by checking census records, birth, death and marriage records, and church or parish records. This can be done by mail, unless you are planning an overseas visit to the ancestral homeland to do your investigation in person. Genealogical libraries have many publications devoted to the various foreign countries and the methods that can be used for research in each one. These publications include the names of genealogical societies that specialize in particular geographic locations and the names and addresses of most of the overseas archives, public offices, libraries, and various other historical sources you can contact for information to assist you in that country. If language is a barrier, you might request the name and address of a local genealogist who, for a fee, will do the research for you.

If, however, you intend to conduct your own correspondence with overseas contacts, it is important to remember to enclose international postal reply coupons, which can be purchased at any post office, with your request for information. You will need to send two coupons along with a self-addressed envelope for air mail, otherwise your reply may take as long as two months to arrive. If you need to send fees for special research, use international money orders from the post office or international bank drafts issued by your own bank.

There are several ways to initiate your foreign research. Most countries today have some sort of bureau of vital statistics either at the local or national level. Start by contacting the one, if any, in the overseas village or town that your ancestor's immigration records indicate as his point of origin, requesting any vital statistics they may have on him. If you can pinpoint your forebear to a particular parish in a specific town, you could also write to whoever is in charge of the church records there, asking for any information they have on any marriages, baptisms, and burials under your ancestor's surname during the particular period of interest.

You will find some countries, such as the British Isles, have very extensive registration of vital records as well as many excellent sources for parish records as do Germany, the Netherlands, and some of the Scandinavian nations. Unfortunately, some of these countries also have had borders that have changed drastically from time to time due to wars, economic problems and political upheavals. Finding records in these areas can be, at times, difficult or even completely unsuccessful.

In Europe, in particular, three major events occurred in the past that affected the destinies of millions of people. These were: the collapse of the vast Austro-Hungarian Empire in 1918-19, involving, but not confined to, the Austrians, Croats, Czechs, Germans, Hungarians, Italians, and Romanians; the breakup of the Ottoman Empire between 1830-1913, affecting the populations of Europe, Asia, and Africa and including Albania, parts of Greece, and the Greek Islands; and the division of Germany and the loss of its territories in 1946 following the end of World War II, which involved parts of Germany and the countries of Poland, Czechoslovakia, and Hungary.

Tracing ancestors who lived in these areas—and most of Europe has been influenced by these changes—can be a laborious and frustrating experience. If you find yourself in this position and do not know who to contact, write to the embassy in Washington, D.C. of the country in question, assuming, of course, it is a nation with which the U.S. enjoys reciprocal diplomatic relations. Request any assistance they can give you on organizations or societies that can help with genealogical research in their nation. Some of the embassies even have literature or pamphlets on how to do genealogical research in their country that they will supply on request.

Iron curtain countries, as a general rule, do not particularly encourage genealogical research in their nations, although even they must find it necessary to keep vital records and census counts of their citizenry. Some of these nations apparently will allow limited access to their records while others will not. And while most of these countries do not allow much written word to reach the outside world, there are those who have visited such places as China, Poland, and Czechoslovakia and have conducted family research quite successfully.

The former Union of Soviet Socialist Republic, which once consisted of fifteen separate republics including Russia and the Ukraine, was once totally uncommunicative as to genealogical inquiries regarding any of these countries. All records were under the jurisdiction of the police authority and, as such, were neither allowed to be filmed nor released to the outside world. However, with the recent dissolution of the Communistic USSR and the subsequent forming of most of these republics into a new, more liberal Commonwealth of Independent States, one can hope today for a freer, more open exchange of genealogical information between these nations and the rest of the free world.

CHAPTER 14

Black Genealogy

> Slavery in all of its forms, in all of its degrees, is a violation of divine law, and a degradation of human nature.
>
> —JACQUES BRISSOT

Of all the many immigrants who have flocked to America's shores seeking a new or better way of life, there was one race of people who had been kidnapped and forced to make the journey to the New World. These unhappy immigrants were the black people. Mostly from West Africa, they had been captured either by European slavers or by enemy African tribes during warfare. Taken away by slave ship, they were destined to be sold on the auction blocks of the early Americas.

It has been said that only about five percent of the slaves brought to the New World actually arrived on the mainland of colonial America. Many never survived the long perilous trip from Africa, dying of privation, disease, abuse, and, in some cases, suicide. Still others had been separated from their family members by sale in the slave marts of the ports of South America and the Caribbean.

African slave trade began around the fifteenth century and, at first, was intended to fill what was a minor labor shortage in such countries as Spain and Portugal. Only after the colonization of the territories of Mexico and Peru and the American settlements in

North America, was there an increased demand for black slave labor. The enslavement or hiring of the local aborigines had not worked; the Indians either refused to work or their ranks had been rapidly decimated by the white man's diseases.

At first the blacks sold to the European slavers were either African prisoners of war taken by enemy tribes or convicted criminals. But by the sixteenth century, the need for slave labor had so drastically increased that some African kings resorted to kidnapping or raids on villages to supply the demand of these traffickers in human misery. Soon, the European slavers began assisting in the kidnappings as slave trading became more and more lucrative.

The importation of black slaves to work in the early American colonies began around the middle of the seventeenth century, but was not in full swing until the end of the century. By the beginning of the eighteenth century, black slave labor comprised most of the agricultural work force in the American South. In 1808 the importing of black slaves from Africa was declared illegal, and afterwards only those born into slavery in America were added to the country's slave population.

Researching a black ancestor who came to colonial America in this fashion is understandably difficult. These people were allowed no personal identities in their new lives, possessing only the first names given to them by their captors who usually refused to use their African names, probably because they could not pronounce them. Only much later, when they became a free people at the end of the Civil War, did they take last names and acquire their own identities and personal records.

Until that time, record keeping for a slave was more concerned with his status as the personal property of the plantation owner than it was with the slave as an individual. Statistics pertaining to births, deaths, and marriages were not considered important to the slave owner and so were not maintained. Usually the only documents referring to slaves, specifically, were wills or tax records that sometimes listed a slave in an inventory. There were also manumission records that were written statements made by a master giving his slave formal freedom. Sometimes these records were kept by the owner's family, but they can also be found sometimes in the state archives or in the National Archives in Washington, D.C.

Under these circumstances one would assume that tracing a

black ancestor back to his pre-Civil War existence would be nearly impossible. However, there is one man who accomplished this feat successfully. Alex Haley recounts in his book, *Roots*, the story of his own genealogical research that started with stories told to him, as a child, by an aged grandmother. He details the many painstaking steps he took in order to be able to finally discover and visit in person the native village of his original African ancestor. This book, although a fictionalized account, is a tribute to one man's unswerving dedication to the challenge of discovering his birthright and heritage.

Genealogy in the United States for black families before the Civil War can be somewhat difficult to research for all of the above reasons. In the National Archives, for example, records of black individuals are mostly interspersed among various others without an indication of race. It is only in the census of 1870 that all blacks were enumerated by name. Free blacks who were heads of households were enumerated by name in censuses from 1790 to 1840 and the names of all free household members were included in the 1850 and 1860 censuses. Slaves were listed in total number or recorded in age and sex categories in censuses of 1790 through 1860. The 1790 census rolls tell not only the names of the free heads of the house, but also indicates how many of these free blacks had slaves of their own. Occasionally, a free black was able to purchase a relative such as a child, husband, or wife.

Blacks have served in all of the wars of the United States dating back to the Revolutionary War. They fought in the Civil War, even serving with the Confederate military forces as well as with the Union troops. The National Archives military records do not usually show race, but there are some separate records that do. For example, when the British evacuated New York in 1783, they took with them many slaves. Lists of those who left with the British were made so that reparation could be made to the former owners under the Treaty of Paris signed in 1783. These lists, called Inspection Rolls, give the names, sex, age, and physical description of each individual. The lists are available for review at the National Archives.

Research for black families follows much the same pattern as it does for others. The census, military service, pension, bounty land, passenger lists, and other records that are important to genealogists are just as pertinent to black family researchers. Some special records do reflect organizations that were formed by the federal government to help blacks after the Civil War.

One such organization was the Freedman's Bureau, created by an act of 1865 and organized, in part, to help slaves make the transition to citizenship in the United States. The bureau was most active from 1865 to 1868 helping blacks legalize slave marriages, witnessing labor contracts, providing food, clothes, and transportation to destitute freedmen and refugees, and relocating them to other parts of the country. In 1869 most of the work of the Freedmen's Bureau was finished and it was abolished in 1872 and all its remaining business turned over to the Freedman's Branch, Office of the Adjutant General.

Other records in the National Archives include manumission records and emancipation papers. In 1862 slavery was abolished in

Figure 30: Typical Slave Ship

the District of Columbia and former slaves could petition for their freedom if their masters did not free them on a voluntary basis. The schedules of those who filed are listed in the emancipation papers. Manumission papers are concerned with masters who voluntarily freed their slaves. Both types of records are on microfilm and arranged chronologically. There are also six volumes of unmicrofilmed manumission and emancipation papers for the years 1821 to 1862, arranged alphabetically by owner, guardian, trustee, or administrator.

In regard to the early slave trade, the National Archives has slave manifests from the U.S. Customs Service of a few of the ships that brought slaves to the United States before it was declared illegal. Masters of ships carrying slaves were required to submit a manifest of these slaves with such information as given name, sex, age, and height. Also included were the names of the shipper and to whom the slave was destined. Because there are no surnames, these lists are of limited value for genealogical research. One would have to know when, where, and by whom the slave was sold before any information could be found.

Other records in the National Archives have to do with the return of Africans rescued from slave vessels bound for the United States to reception centers at Sherbro Island, Cape Mesurado, and Liberia, West Africa. These records also discuss the temporary placement of Africans in the southern states of the United States. A census roll of the colonization of Liberia by blacks sent by the American Colonization Society and its Auxiliaries in 1843 is also on record at the National Archives and available for review.

The National Archives also has a number of important special lists to offer the black researcher. One of them is Special List 34, *List of Free Black Heads of Families in the First Census of the United States, 1790,* which disclosed the names of the approximately 4,000 free black heads of families listed in the general census of that date. This list is easy to use as the names are alphabetized under each state, and includes all the members of a family. It is especially beneficial for black research because until 1850 the general federal census had no special provisions for blacks. If a racial designation was noted at all, it was usually as "other persons," a classification that also included Native Americans.

For those who wish to research a black Revolutionary War

ancestor, the National Archives offers Special List 36, *List of Black Servicemen Compiled from the War Department Collection of Revolutionary War Records,* which relates to the known, or presumed to be black servicemen who fought in that war. This list was compiled from three sources in the War Department collection of Revolutionary War records and references, in addition, further information regarding these sources. This list is alphabetized by name and also indicates the home state of the serviceman, information vital for continued research into the military records of the National Archives.

Other special records in the National Archives pertaining to blacks include the records of the Bureau of Refugees, Freedmen, and Abandoned Lands; commonly known as the Freedman's Bureau. Record Group 105 of this agency contains the records of the commissioner's office in Washington, D.C., as well as those of the various field offices of the bureau. The information found in the group of records include freedmen's marriages, scattered state census records, labor contracts, and school records. Although a lack of indexing of names and the particular arrangement of the records can prohibit easy access, they can sometimes provide a diligent researcher with much valuable information on a black ancestor.

Another group of records of the Freedmen's Bureau have to do with the depositions made in branches of the Freedmen's Savings and Trust Company, incorporated in 1865 primarily for the benefit of former slaves. The bank branches maintained registers of the depositors, mostly black, in which can be found the depositor's account number, his name, date and place of birth, occupation, residency, and extensive information regarding his family members. Sometimes the name of a former master or mistress and plantation is indicated, which can be useful to those tracing back to a slave ancestor.

These records are found in Record Group 101, *Records of the Comptroller of the Currency,* in the National Archives. Unfortunately, the records are indexed by account number, not by name, making effective research more time-consuming. The registrars are arranged alphabetically by state; the entries are listed alphabetically by city, and then chronologically by date the account was opened. To use this agency's records, which have been reproduced on microfilm as *Registers of Signatures of Depositors in Branches of the Freedmen's*

Savings and Trust Company, 1865-1874, (M816, 27 rolls) a researcher would need to first know the city of the researched subject's account. Once you have obtained this, you can check the indexes, located in the same group of records, which are arranged first by state, by branch city, and then by initial or surname.

Although investigating the records of the Freedmen's Savings and Trust Company can be tedious, it is also invaluable as a research source. Because signatures could not be utilized, as the majority of the blacks of that day were illiterate, most bank tellers were diligent in recording all of the biographical information needed to identify a depositor. As a result, the depositor's card can reveal a rich bonanza of information concerning a black ancestor.

Most of the information mentioned so far has to do only with those blacks who first entered the United States as slaves. It is important, however, when researching black genealogy, to remember there were a considerable number of free blacks in the United States during its colonial period. Among them was a black community that existed in New York as far back as 1640. Most entered the county from the ports of the Caribbean where there were many free blacks, or from Angola in Portuguese West Africa, which, paradoxically, was one of the main centers for early African slave trade. Many of these free Angolans appear to have settled in New York between the 1630s and the 1730s around Manhattan Island. Others settled in areas of New England as well as in other early American colonies.

Researching an early, free pre-Civil War ancestor involves much the same techniques employed in seeking the records of any other early American ancestor. Much information can usually be found among the records of the general population such as census or military records, although some states did take special censuses of free blacks. Other censuses included the names of free blacks in the general population count, and indicated the individual's race next to his name, a fact that can be of considerable value to a black family researcher.

A check with *A Guide to Genealogical Research in the National Archives* will indicate where these and other records referring to blacks can be found in the National Archives and how to research them. Also, many libraries, both genealogical and regular, have publications relating to black history and culture that may be of interest to black genealogical researchers wishing to establish a link with their original immigrant ancestors.

Two, in particular, of these publications are of the utmost importance for your research. The first, *The Directory of Afro-American Resources,* edited by Walter Schatz and published in 1970 by R.W. Bowker, lists over 2,000 American institutions, among which are libraries, public and private agencies, and civil rights organizations. The book includes the full name, address, and telephone number of each organization, along with a full description of its collection.

The second work is a book called *Blacks in Selected Newspapers, Censuses and Other Sources: An Index to Names and Subjects,* compiled by James de T. Abajian and published by the G.K. Hall Company in 1977. This volume is an extensive guide to black names and activities in the nineteenth and twentieth centuries and indicates the published records in which they can be found. Some of these sources include newspapers and periodicals as well as state and federal census records and city directories, all invaluable to black research.

Another vital source of information for black researchers are the records of the black churches. These churches, which have been a focal point in black society, contain files on marriages, baptisms, and burials. They can offer, in addition, the removal letters that were issued to a church member when he transferred his membership, an excellent means of tracing the movements of a mobile black ancestor.

Churches such as the African Methodist, Baptist, and Catholic have kept excellent records even up to modern times. The historic Christ Church in Philadelphia is famous for its early members both black and white, which include George Washington, seven signers of the Declaration of Independence, and Benjamin Franklin, who is buried in its cemetery. The Mother Bethel African Methodist Church, founded by Richard Allen in 1787, is the oldest black church in America.

All of these churches kept detailed membership records that may still be in existence today either at the church or at a historical society or university. Contact the church's pastor directly for help in ascertaining the location of these records.

Chapter 15

Native Americans

I am indeed Earth's child.
Absolutely I am Earth's child.
—Navajo Song of the Earth

Although the vast North American continent had been visited many times in its historical past by travelers from other lands, credit for being this country's first citizens has been given to a group of indigenous people who are thought to be the ancestors of the race known to us today as American Indians. Traces of these aboriginal people can be seen in such areas as Canada's Yukon territory. Scrapers found there date back to about 25,000 B.C. and artifacts found in an early Indian settlement near Pittsburgh have been carbon dated to around 17,000 B.C.

The earliest skeletal remains of these ancient wanderers were found near Midland, Texas, and are less than 12,000 years old. The few skulls of these people that were unearthed indicate to present-day authorities that they were a slender graceful type, not particularly identifiable with any of today's known races of people. The thinking of most modern day anthropologists is that today's racial differences have only evolved during the past 20,000 years.

At present, there are a number of modern American Indian types, which can vary within certain groups and in different areas. Some are short and stocky, like the pueblo Indians of the southwest, while others are tall and slender like the plains Indians of the

Midwest. They do, however, all have one characteristic in common. They are all of a distinctly individual racial category, all unmistakably members of the American Indian race.

Their early American ancestors apparently first entered North America by way of the Bering land bridge many centuries ago, perhaps between 30,000 and 8,000 B.C. when the land now under the Bering Straits, connecting Alaska with Siberia, stood high and dry. Most anthropologists seem to concur that these first inhabitants of the North American continent were Asiatic men and women from Siberia. It is believed they first entered the new continent through Alaska after the Ice Age had locked up the world's water and the oceans had receded from the shores, leaving such areas as the Bering Straits, ordinarily under water, as dry land.

Once in North America, the wanderers eventually split up, each following food sources of game and vegetables in his own way. The wide area of land mass traveled by these early prehistoric immigrants eventually resulted in a proliferation of a number of separate and markedly different Indian cultures.

The diversity of their cultures can be seen in the variety of the different, spoken Indian languages. According to linguistic experts, by the time the white man arrived, there were at least twelve (some say as many as eighteen) distinct Indian languages in existence with many variations and dialects. All were as different from one another as Russian is from English.

For these Indians were of an oral culture and eloquence in speech was part of their heritage. Children learned their history from tribal legends and tales told by elders around campfires. The art of oratory was practiced by all the great chieftains, especially on occasions when persuasive rhetoric was needed to stir their people or to negotiate a treaty with the white man.

Although verbally fluent, these native Americans did not have a written language. As a result, they communicated with each other only with speech, smoke signals, or with a graceful hand language referred to by some admiring onlookers as "poetry in motion." Some eastern tribes, such as the Iroquois, used wampum belts for memory aids, but the use of more extensive devices such as picture glyphs used by the South American Indians, were not known to the North American plains Indians. To document special historical events, buffalo skins with drawings were used by such tribes as the

Sioux. The records on these hides, done in a kind of pictorial shorthand, were called "winter counts," probably because winter indicated a whole year to them. Many years could be depicted on these skins by the drawings of major events during those years. Sometimes the skins were over hundred years old before they were completed. But it was not until 1821 that an actual Indian alphabet was invented by a Cherokee leader of mixed blood named Sequoyah, for whom the California redwoods were named. Sequoyah, who knew no English, devised this alphabet, comprised of 86 characters, by borrowing some of the characters from English and making up the rest. In spite of the many characters, the alphabet was easily learned by the Cherokee and soon thousands of them could read and write. This development enabled Sequoyah to produce, in Cherokee, such publications as newspapers, the Bible, and many books about Indian life and culture.

The lack of any early written records for Native Americans unfortunately makes genealogical research for an Indian ancestor extremely difficult if it is to predate the coming of the white man. The early American Indian, apparently, felt no necessity to develop an educational system such as that used by the Europeans with its emphasis on the ability to read and write. To the Indian, the young needed to be trained only in such practical matters as how to endure heat, cold, and hunger, how to build a shelter, or kill an enemy. These skills were handed down from generation to generation, all without ever knowing of, or using, a written language.

Such tribes as the Navajo have for countless generations passed their legends along to their young in the language of the "Dineh," or the People, a language still spoken today. These legends, which tell of their sacred mountains, and of First Man and First Woman, have recently been printed in English.

The Indian has adopted many useful aspects of the white man's culture, such as the knowledge of animal husbandry, the use of firearms and the art of silversmithing, to name a few. But there is one element of European society with which the Indian culture has throughout history run counter to, and that is the white man's concept of land ownership. Unfortunately, the result of the divergent points of view has probably been responsible for the greatest amount of conflict between the two cultures.

Before the Europeans arrived, American Indians lived in tribes or extended family groups and land ownership was communal. In cultures such as the Iroquois, for example, the land could be tilled or hunted by individuals, but the bounty was shared by all. Even their housing was communal and the concept of private property was of little importance to them. To the Indian, the land and its resources were to be shared, not owned individually. He believed the earth was for the use of all and belonged to no one. Some tribes even regarded the earth as the mother of all life and therefore to sell "Mother Earth" would have been considered sacrilegious. To the Navajo, it was "Mother Earth, Father Sky," a phrase that indicated the feeling of kinship the Indian felt for his native land.

European culture, however, was based, to some extent, upon the concept that private land ownership was an important aspect of society. Because the Indians did not exploit their land in a way that whites traditionally did, it was apparently thought by the Europeans that the Indians did not need or properly utilize the vast lands that they occupied. Therefore, to confiscate the Indian land was both expedient and fitting. With such a difference in their respective philosophies, the clash between the two cultures was inevitable.

Although conflict between the red man and the white dated from the very beginning of European colonization in America, it had been expressed mostly through tribal warfare or displacement of the Indians as the white man pushed onward across the new nation. However, in 1830, President Andrew Jackson sponsored the first of the legislative acts designed to actually force the Indians from their land. The Indian Removal Act authorized the relocating of Indian tribes east of the Mississippi River to new settlements on land in the west. This relocation was undertaken even though the Supreme Court had ruled that the forced removal of the Indians without their approval would be illegal.

As the frontier moved toward the west, more and more Indians were displaced as land-hungry settlers and avid gold seekers pressed across Indian lands. There were Indian uprisings as treaties were broken and other treaties replaced them. The divesting of the red men of their ancestral lands continued as they were constantly moved westward by the federal government to reservations on specific land designated for Indian occupation.

Because of the lack of early written records for Native

Americans, most material of any genealogical value available for research involves records of Indians and their interaction with the United States government and the Bureau of Indian Affairs. The Bureau of Indian Affairs was created by the federal government in 1824 for the purpose of acting as a trustee for Indian property held in trust by the United States and to assist in providing education, health, and welfare services for the Indians.

The BIA was originally administered by the War Department, a policy reflecting the government thinking in those days of the Indians as "hostile." In 1849, however, responsibility for the administration of the bureau was transferred to the Department of the Interior where it remains to this day.

Nowadays under a U.S. policy of Indian self-determination, elected tribal governments run their own reservations with assistance from the Bureau of Indian Affairs. The bureau's present-day main goal is to support the tribes' efforts by providing them with technical assistance and special programs and services as well as administering and managing over 50 million acres of land held by the U.S. for Indians. The BIA also concentrates on providing the tribes with opportunities to be more self-governing, moving away, to a degree, from daily involvement in tribal matters.

Because of this continuous interaction between the bureau and the Indian tribes, the records of the BIA in the National Archives and Records Center in Washington, D.C., and its eleven archives branches house an immense collection of federal-Indian records. The Washington D.C., office holds the largest amount of original Indian material, while the regional archives centers contain some original and some microfilmed copies of the records. Pertinent material includes papers relating to Indian treaties, annuity payments, tribal census rolls, and maps of Indian lands and reservations. These records are available for public review in the National Archives and most can be copied for a small fee.

The Office of the Bureau of Indian Affairs is very helpful to American Indian researchers and will assist you any way it can. However, to effectively use the vast amount of material in the records of the BIA or any other American Indian collection, you will need to know your ancestors' tribal affiliations. You must also have this information to ascertain your own Indian ancestry if this is also one of your goals.

Although not always easily determined, there are things you can do if you do not have enough information to identify your tribal ties. For example, by conducting a basic genealogical research of your Indian forebears, paying particular attention to their dates and places of birth, marriages, and death, you may be able to detect a pattern of their early movements. If a certain geographic area seems to be predominant, researching the Indian tribes known to have once been in that locale while checking any present-day Indian reservations still in that vicinity, may narrow your search to just one or two Indian tribes.

There are a number of useful publications that can also aid your research if you are having problems determining your tribal ancestry. One publication, *Indian Tribes of North America,* by John R. Swanton discusses the difficulty with the word, "tribe," and attempts to clarify the term as it applies to Native American groups and subgroups. The book is arranged alphabetically by state and then by tribal name and covers the history and location for all major tribes of North America.

Another valuable reference source for American Indians is the *Handbook of American Indians North of Mexico,* by Frederick Webb Hodge. The important two-volume work lists alphabetically the names of North American Indian tribes and offers a useful cross reference of the variant spelling or other names of the tribes along with a brief history of each.

Once you think you have established your ancestors' tribe or tribes, you can either write directly to the tribal headquarters or to the BIA agency located nearest the reservations. Another useful source to contact would be the Bureau of Indian Affairs, Branch of Tribal Enrollment, 1849 C. St. N.W., Washington, D.C. 20408. Give them your ancestors' names and ask if they appear on any official tribal rolls or census lists.

Whatever agency you contact, be sure to give them all spellings of the names including any forebears listed with more than one name. Before the coming of the white man, an Indian child was given only one name, although he sometimes acquired a nickname. When the first federal census of Indians was taken in 1885, the white enumerators usually spelled the strange-sounding Indian names phonetically for lack of any established methods of translating them to English. To compound the problem, when by an act of 1884, annual Indian censuses became a federal requirement, it was deemed necessary for the Indian to also have a last name so one was usually invented by the Indian family. As a consequence, from 1885 to 1940, the last year of the census, the annual Indian census listed either the traditional Indian name, the newly given English name, or, in the case of early censuses, both.

Annual Indian censuses are a valuable source of genealogical material, especially the first so-called transitional census of 1885-1890, containing as it does, both the Indian and given name of the individual. By researching these census lists, you may be able to establish a relationship between your Indian forebear's given English name and his original Indian one. Microfilmed copies of the rolls are available in the National Archives as *Indian Census Rolls, M595.* This census is discussed in detail later in the chapter.

There were certain problems with the annual Indian census. Because the censuses were taken only of those Indians living on certain reservations at a given time, many were overlooked. Also, not all Indians living on a reservation were members of the tribe, as spouses usually belonged to another tribe. Some tribes were not enumerated at all. For example, there were no census rolls submitted for the Five Civilized Tribes of Oklahoma who had earlier emigrated from east of the Mississippi River to lands in the West.

After the reorganization of tribal government in 1933, the annual Indian census was replaced by the more comprehensive tribal enrollment record. Because only enrolled members of the tribes are eligible to receive the benefits and rights of the tribe, the resulting enrollment lists are a detailed legal description of each member. The tribe, itself, determines its own membership criteria, although the U.S. can also establish tribal membership. Enrollment lists are maintained by the enrollment officer of the regional BIA in conjunction with the tribal council.

Who is considered an Indian? It depends upon whom you ask. To a census taker, an Indian is anyone who declares himself or herself to be one. The Bureau of Indian Affairs requires that for eligibility an Indian must be a member of a federally recognized tribe and be of one-fourth or more ancestry. Although Aleuts, Eskimos, and Indians of Alaska are also eligible for BIA benefits, most of BIA services and programs are limited to Indians living on or near federal reservations.

How does one become a member of a recognized tribe? Tribal membership requirements are determined by the enrollment criteria of each tribe, which can vary. Usually you must present documented proof of your right to be enrolled in the tribe. Descent from an ancestor who was a tribal member plus a certain quantum of Indian blood are the usual requirements. This, too, can vary. While some tribes require only a trace of Indian blood, others may require as much as one-half.

Even most unrecognized tribes, that is, those who chose not to join a reservation at the time of treaty-making and therefore are not recognized by the federal government as legal entities, have some membership requirements. Most of these groups have today formed themselves into an organization with elected officers and are requesting formal federal recognition. Information on these tribes may be obtained either from the tribal headquarters or the BIA agency working with the tribe.

There is an excellent booklet put out by the Bureau of Indian Affairs called *American Indians Today* in which the BIA attempts to answer some of its most frequently asked questions. This pamphlet also contains lists of source material and recommended readings for American Indian researchers. You can obtain this publication and other material relating to Indians by writing to the BIA office nearest you, or to the bureau's main office in Washington, D.C. You will find a list of the Bureau of Indian Affairs area offices in Appendix D. Address your inquiries to: Area Director, Bureau of Indian Affairs, followed by the address.

Another useful reading guide is the publication *Genealogical Research in the National Archives.* Available in most libraries, this book is an invaluable source of information on the type and scope of BIA material in the National Archives and its branches. It also indicates which Federal Archives and Record Center (FARC) has the various tribal records kept by the field personnel who maintained personal contact with the Indians. Although there are some pre-federal Indian records in the National Archives, the official BIA records begin in 1824, the year of its establishment.

Some of the earliest records concerning Indians in the National Archives are those relating to the Indian Removal Act of 1830. They offer information about the relocation of some eastern tribes known as the Five Civilized Tribes, so-called to differentiate them from the buffalo-hunting tribes of the plains Indians. The five tribes involved in the Indian Removal Act were the Cherokees, Chickasaws, Choctaws, Creeks, and Seminoles, who had been persuaded, one might say, to leave their ancestral lands in the East and accept lands west of the Mississippi River.

These records, which cover the period 1839 through 1852, are arranged by agency and tribe and include some Indian censuses taken before emigration. The censuses are mostly of the Creek nation, taken in 1832, and of the Cherokee nation, taken in 1835, and occasionally reveal only the names of the heads of the family. Some of the other records, however, also indicate the number of persons by age and sex in each family and, on occasion, the original place of residence for each head of the family. There are also muster rolls of the migrating Indians, arranged chronologically, and therefore not of such value to the genealogical researcher unless the actual date of the Indian emigration is known.

One very valuable set of records found in the National Archives is the annuity payrolls that resulted when the United States, in keeping with treaties made with the Indians, agreed to pay certain sums or goods to heads of the Indian families. The rolls are usually listed by tribes and then chronologically and show such things as the names of the heads of the family and the name and sex of each family member as well as the amount paid to them. These records were usually kept from 1848 through 1940.

From time to time, the BIA took a number of school censuses, listing Indian children, their ages, birth places, and their parents' names. In 1860, the regular federal census added a category called "Indians taxed" that was concerned with Indians who had left the reservations and were living among the whites. However, it was not until 1890 that the enumeration of all Indians on or off the reservations was included in the general federal census.

In 1885, by special act of Congress, each Indian agent was directed to compile a list of Indians in his charge. The resulting census rolls are listed by Indian agency, by tribe, and then by year. These rolls show the name (both Indian and English), sex, age, and relationship of the Indian to the head of the house. Unfortunately, the lists were not alphabetized before 1916, making research difficult as one must scan all of the tribes listed. The compilation policy was continued up until 1940 for most of the tribes.

In 1887, after the settlement of the Indian Wars with the United States, Congress passed the General Allotment Act for the purpose of breaking up tribal reservation holdings into individual ownership. This was apparently done for the quicker assimilation of the Indian into the general population. It was thought that by issuing an Indian his own personal plot of land he could sustain himself as a farmer, an aspiration that unfortunately did not always prove feasible. These records contain a great deal of genealogical information. The Dawes Commission arranged the land divisions, preparing census rolls for eligible Indians, listing name, age, sex, degree of Indian blood, and the roll number of each individual. The original rolls are called, "Final Rolls of Citizens and Freemen of the Five Civilized Tribes in Indian Territory."

There are other land allotment records found in the archives regarding extinguishment of tribal title and conversion to individual Indian title. Arranged by tribe and then by enrollment number, the contents usually include applications for allotment, plat maps of the land and register of names of allottees and descriptions of their allotments.

In 1902, eastern Cherokee Indians filed three suits against the U.S. government for funds due them by the Treaties of 1835, 1836, and 1845. The resulting enrollment of the Cherokees during 1907-08 is considered one of the most extensive ever made because the Indians were required to prove their descent from the original eastern Cherokee tribes in order to share in the over one million dollars awarded to them by the courts. The case files are microfilmed as "Eastern Cherokee Applications of the U.S. Court of Claims" and can be found in the National Archives. This action was just one of many to come authorizing the Indians to reclaim by legal action many of the lands that had been taken away from them illegally.

By an act of June 2, 1924, all Indians born in the territory of the United States were declared citizens and could still maintain their tribal membership. Prior to this, Indians had received citizenship only through federal statue or treaties with the United States. Because Indians had participated in all of the wars involving the United States, it has been suggested that belated granting of citizenship was an expression of gratitude from the government to the non-citizen Indians who fought in defense of this country.

At any rate, in 1924, they were finally included in the Fourteenth amendment to the Constitution that guaranteed national citizenship to all persons born or naturalized in the United States.

The Dawes Allotment Act stayed in effect until 1934, when under President Franklin D. Roosevelt, it was finally repealed by the passing of the Indian Reorganization Act, which gave the Indians back their capacity to act as corporate entities and allowed them to again acquire land for Indian use only. In addition, it set up a revolving loan fund designed to stimulate economic development for the tribes, while providing for more extensive education for Indians and encouraging them to have a greater involvement in Indian services and affairs.

Although the publication *Guide to the National Archives of the United States* covers much of the BIA material located in the National Archives, another publication compiled in 1982 by Edward E. Hill, *Guide to Records in the National Archives Relating to American Indians,* is invaluable for more extensive genealogical research of BIA's Indian collection. In this publication, Mr. Hill discusses the administrative structure of the BIA while supplying more specific description as to the locations of certain Indian record series in the National Archives.

Although the BIA's Indian collection is impressive, there are many other sources of Indian records to investigate. One such collection is in the Smithsonian Institute, Department of Anthropology, 10th Street and Constitution Avenue N.W., Washington, D.C. 20560. The Institute's Handbook Office is preparing a comprehensive 20-volume series on North American Indians entitled *Handbook of North American Indians.* At least nine volumes of this series have already been published and are available through public and genealogical libraries. You can write directly to the Smithsonian Institute for literature on the type of Indian material available for review in its collection.

The Library of Congress, 10 First Street, S.E., Washington, D.C. 20540, has an extensive amount of genealogical material that includes books, photographs, manuscripts, and other sources for your Indian research. Reference librarians are on hand to assist you to use its general and special American Indian collections.

There are also private record collections that can offer much to an American Indian researcher. The Oklahoma Historical Society in Oklahoma City has one of the most extensive and well-indexed American Indian collections around. As was mentioned earlier, the LDS Library in Salt Lake City, Utah, contains extensive microfilmed records concerning both the eastern and western North American Indian tribes. Information on these collections can be obtained by writing directly to the libraries.

Other literature regarding North American Indian tribes can be found in both genealogical and regular public libraries. Occasionally one can find literary works that deal particularly with certain notable American Indians, exceptional men and women who have made lasting contributions to the history and shaping of the young country.

Their ancestors were the ancient wanderers who came to this new land without the fanfare or sense of historical happening and adventure that later pioneers would experience. Long ago these early people crossed an arctic bridge to venture into an unknown, unexplored, and sometimes perilous world. As the first Americans learned to survive in that world, so did their progeny learn to survive in this one. From the very first prehistoric traveler to set a timorous foot on this strange new land, down to his modern-day descendant, the American Indian has earned a well-deserved right to the title of America's first citizen.

CHAPTER 16

Heraldry

TO ALL AND SINGULAR
to whom these Presents shall come . . .

Heraldry, the use of a decorative and symbolic, family-identifying coat of arms, is an ancient, colorful, and some say anachronistic throwback to medieval Europe, that still continues to be in vogue. Its everlasting endurance and continuing popularity throughout the ages might seem puzzling to some, but an examination of the appeal of heraldry could explain to some extent the reason for its survival to the present day.

Heraldry is many things to many people. It holds interest for the antiquarian a well as for the historian and is sought after eagerly by a would-be armiger (one who is entitled to bear heraldic arms) for the honor that the possession of a coat of arms bestows upon a deserving recipient. It has also been described by some authorities as a precise science, one that combines the characteristics of beauty with the practicality of usage.

The study of heraldry is also considered, by some, a study of Gothic art form, originating long ago in Europe for utilitarian reasons, but surviving to this day because of its exquisite visual appeal and the emotional power of its symbolism concerning as it does family and honor. It is a prestigious insignia of a gentleman, identifying a man with an illustrious ancestor who had been awarded the original coat of arms through service to the Crown.

T. WOODCOCK
SOMERSET HERALD

The College of Arms,
Queen Victoria Street,
London EC4V 4BT
Tel:- 01 236 3634

30th May 1985

Ms. B.A.Underwood,
2508 Rio Bravo Circle,
Sacramento,
Calif. 95826.

Dear Ms. Underwood,

Thank you for your letter of 30th April which has come to me as Officer in Waiting.

Honorary Grants of personal Armorial Bearings are made to eminent Americans who can prove and register here their descent in an unbroken male line from someone who was a subject of the British Crown. This means descent from someone living in America before Independence or from a subsequent immigrant from a country subject to the British Crown.

Grants are not therefore made to eminent Americans who cannot prove this descent.

Application for an Honorary Grant which is recorded in the College records in the same way as any other Grant and which is made by Letters Patent of the Kings of Arms can be made either directly to one of the thirteen Officers of Arms or alternatively by writing to the Officer in Waiting who is one of the six Heralds or four Pursuivants who is responsible for dealing with all general enquiries on a weekly rota basis. The cost of recording the Pedigree back to an emigrant ancestor depends on the number of generations recorded. Evidence must be provided in the form of certificates of birth, marriage and death, census returns, testamentary records, family Bible entries, etc., to substantiate the descent. At present the cost of drafting, examination and registration of a Pedigree going back to the late-18th century would probably be in the region of £200. The fees on a personal Grant of Arms and a Crest are at present £840, though this will probably be increased this year. It is also open to a Grantee to have a Grant of a heraldic Badge. If granted in the same Letters Patent this costs a further £250. A Badge can be granted by a subsequent Patent in which case the cost is £350.

The same tests for eminence are applied to all personal Grantees and for some centuries a University degree, professional qualification, or civil or military commission, has been considered in normal circumstances to satisfy the conditions as would particular eminence in one field.

If I can help you any further please address any future correspondence to me in person in order to avoid delay.

Yours sincerely,

Thomas Woodcock

T. Woodcock
Somerset Herald

Figure 31: Letter outlining qualifications for obtaining honorary grants of armorial bearings (coat of arms)

(The College of Arms, London)

During medieval times, heraldry was originally conceived as a system of identifying an individual by means of hereditary markings placed upon a shield known as a coat of arms. It was intended to be a method during battle whereby the ordinary man-at-arms could readily identify and follow his leader. A coat of arms could also be placed upon a seal to identify the participants in such business transactions as the signing of formal documents or contracts. In that time, most of those of noble blood were illiterate and the seal was accepted in lieu of a signature.

Heraldry dates back to around the twelfth century and is related to the early development of armor. At first only those of greater nobility used the arms, but soon the lesser nobility, such as knights and gentlemen, adopted their use. These men of quality had in their employ officers of the household called heralds whose duty it was to keep track of their masters' many achievements and accomplishments of glory. It was to the heralds that the task of devising and keeping a record of the arms first fell, hence the term "heraldry."

In the years preceding the wearing of heraldic shields, it was customary for the leader of an army to ride with his face uncovered, protected only by a sort of hood made of chain links. He was easily recognized by his men, but, unfortunately, also by the enemy and thus vulnerable to personal attack from the foe. It has been suggested that had Harold, the last Saxon king of England, been protected by a closed helmet, a development later made possible by the use of heraldic devices, then he might never have been killed at the Battle of Hastings fought in 1066 to protect English soil from the Norman invaders. In the Bayeau tapestry King Harold is depicted lifting his helmet to identify himself, when he was killed due to, some say, his unprotected face. The Normans, with no one to stop them, won the battle and then, under William the Conqueror, went on to defeat England. Had this not happened who knows what direction English (and American) history might have taken?

By the fourteenth century, a principle was adopted in England that no man could wear another's arms, and soon afterward it was also decreed that no man could use a coat of arms without proper authority from the Crown and to be issued only by the Royal Heralds. The coat of arms and the crest, originally worn high above the helmet, were family property and could be passed down to an elder son and later to all of a man's offspring. His sons wore the same arms as the father with small distinguishing differences. Even a man's daughter could display the armorial devices except for the crest and not on a shield since women were not supposed to go into battle. The right to use a family coat of arms even today is handed down from father to sons with only the males entitled to bear the arms.

In heraldic design a full armorial bearing usually consists of a crest, helm, mantling, shield, supporters, and a scroll with a motto. The shield is of the most importance and it is here that the coat of arms was first displayed. It was also embroidered on the surcoat, a garment placed over the armor, thus the reason for the term "coat of arms." It was also placed on the horse's trappings as well as on the banner for all to see. The crest was developed a little later, perhaps for tournaments, and was worn high above the helmet and consisted of such things as feathers or, occasionally, an animal or bird copied from the coat of arms. Also on the shield were the supporters, creatures placed on each side of the armorial shield supposedly holding or "supporting" it. These usually were depicted as living creatures, but could be imaginary such as dragons and monsters.

The most popular animal used was the lion, placed in many different positions, sometimes being "rampant," that is, rearing, or "salient," in the act of springing. The motto, if there is one, is usually placed under the shield, and is generally a brief phrase expressing a sentiment or perhaps a war cry.

The mantling was, at first, a long cloth attached to the helmet that hung down around the shoulders. It was probably originally intended for protection from the hot sun beating down upon the metal of the armor and was in the shape of a cloak. Later, the mantling evolved into such things as feather-like strips, gold tassels, or ermine for royalty.

Heraldry has its own colorful language that is Norman French and Latin, somewhat Anglicized, and written today exactly as it was in the fifteenth century. To "blazon" a coat of arms is to describe it verbally with such technical details that a competent designer can make a correct drawing from it. In describing blazons such terms as the following are used for a partial description of the arms of Sir Winston Churchill: "Sable a lion rampant argent with a canton of the last thereon a cross gules . . ." If a literal translation is applied, per a heraldic glossary, it seems to appear to the untutored eye as ". . . a silver lion, rearing on its left hind leg, next to a small square containing a red cross. . . ."

The evidence of the artistry of heraldry can be seen repeated in many forms in England. It is found in the beauty and grandeur of the stained glass windows in a Gothic church or in the architectural design of a public building. At times, colorful displays of arms and crests can also be seen in the pageantry that accompanies certain state or royal occasions that take place frequently. For the private individual, however, heraldic design is usually confined to such traditional personal items as family silver, glassware, and jewelry.

And so heraldry, with its bright and beautiful designs and merry language, still has an inordinate appeal for many people. The College of Arms in London, England, founded in 1884, is still very actively engaged in researching old claims of those who wish to establish the right to bear an existing coat of arms. Its thirteen Royal Heralds must be genealogists and historians as well as artists and designers. Another occupation of the Royal Heralds has to do with the designing of new armorial bearings for those applicants who are considered worthy of the honor.

In England the right to bear arms is granted in two ways, either by a grant of arms by letters patent, meaning authorized by the Crown, or by armiger, or inheritance by lineal descent from an ancestor to whom a grant was made. Today in England in order to obtain your own coat of arms, you must apply to the College of Arms.

Although a fee is required, money is not the factor considered in the granting of arms to a private citizen. A grant of arms is considered a minor honor and so the recipient must be proven to be a person "worthy and with great integrity," who has not acquired his wealth by any questionable means. He must also be considered a leader in his field, be in a dignified profession such as law or public service, and/or be a university graduate. This same yardstick of respectability applies also to public entities such as cities and large corporations that must display some civic eminence or public leadership in order to qualify. Many corporate bodies apparently desire heraldic insignias as a symbol of stability and traditionalism that a coat of arms implies.

There are some basic differences among the countries that make up Great Britain in regard to obtaining and using a coat of arms. The laws of heraldry in England as well as in Northern Ireland and Wales are based upon the old law of the land. Today, the use of bogus arms can be, and is done, with impunity. Such is not the case in Scotland where the laws regarding heraldry are based upon parliamentary law and therefore can be enforced. There, even an offspring of an armiger must apply to the Lord Lyon for his own set of arms when he reaches the age of maturity and is issued a coat of arms distinctly his own.

Here in the United States there is no law to prohibit the use of any heraldic symbols for decorative purposes. However, to assume that you have the right to use a coat of arms just because someone with your surname has one is incorrect. In order to properly claim a particular heraldic device as your own, you must prove your descent by direct line from an ancestor who was granted one.

This may not be as far-fetched as it seems at first glance. Some authorities have estimated that there were probably around 10,000 armigers in England in the year 1300. These figures have been calculated to produce over 30 million descendants living today who are still entitled to bear the original arms of their ancestors unless there had been considerable intermarrying.

For even if your original American immigrant from the British Isles appeared to be a person of modest means or of yeoman stock, this does not mean that he was not entitled to bear arms. In the past, many of noble blood occasionally suffered financial reverses and were not in a position to apply for and bear the arms rightfully theirs. If you desire to go to the expense of an official investigation, do not be surprised to learn that someone in your present family may still have the right to bear an early ancestor's coat of arms.

If you are interested in investigating your right to use a coat of arms here in the United States, you should contact the New England Historic Genealogical Society in Boston, Massachusetts, which has a large genealogical library with a heraldry department. This organization has investigated many claims by American families as to their rights to heraldic devices and has published a large roll of coats of arms that you can check by writing to the New England Historic Genealogical Society, Committee on Heraldry, Boston, Massachusetts 02116.

Could a citizen of a foreign country, such as America, obtain a *new* coat of arms for himself from the College of Arms in London? The answer is, yes, a citizen from another country can apply for and receive a grant of arms by letters patent, from the College of Arms, as any Briton can, under certain conditions.

This, however, has not always been the case. In the past, England had placed a ban on the issuing of new grants of arms to Americans, a ban that dated from the time of the Revolutionary War of 1776. This ban remained in effect for about 150 years, its removal coinciding with World War I, which America entered as ally of England.

At any rate, an American applying for a grant of arms today must qualify on two points. He must prove descent from a British subject, either one who had been in the colonies at the time of the Revolutionary War, or one who subsequently immigrated from a country subject to the British Crown. He must also qualify in eminence, that is, be deserving of the honor that armorial bearings bestow. The same tests of eminence that apply to a modern Briton also apply to an American. That is, he must possess a university degree or other qualifications such as professional eminence or a civil or military commission.

To obtain further information regarding the granting of new arms for Americans or to research old ones for England, Northern Ireland, and Wales, write to the College of Arms, Queen Victoria Street, London, England. To research a Scottish ancestor, write to the Lord Lyon, Lyon Office, Edinburgh, Scotland. For the Republic of Ireland, contact the Chief Herald of Ireland, Dublin, Ireland.

Many other countries used armorial devices dating back to feudal Christianity times. Contact the Washington, D.C., embassy of the country in question and see if they can assist you. You will probably have a better chance with countries that either still have a monarchy or at least are not vigorously opposed to it as heraldry is still somewhat tied in with royalty. This would indicate that communist countries, for example, would probably not encourage contact for purposes of heraldic research while countries like Belgium, Spain, France, and Japan still have a national interest in all areas of heraldic enterprise.

Many genealogical libraries also have a number of publications dedicated to heraldic research in the various European countries. Most of these books provide considerable information, not only on the background and history of heraldry, but also on whom to write regarding your own heraldic research. Also, some of the reading material referenced in the back of this book can give further detailed information on the proper sources to contact in many European countries.

APPENDIX A

National Archives Branches and Areas Served

WASHINGTON, D.C.
National Archives and Record Service
NNC
Washington, D.C. 20408

BOSTON:
380 Trapelo Rd.
Waltham, MA 021454
Serves Connecticut, Maine, Massachusetts, New Hampshire, Rhode Island, and Vermont.

NEW YORK:
Building 22—MOT Bayonne
Bayonne, NJ 07002
Serves New Jersey, New York, Puerto Rico, and the Virgin Islands.

PHILADELPHIA:
5000 Wissahickon Ave.
Philadelphia, PA 19144
Serves Delaware and Pennsylvania; for the loan of microfilm also serves the District of Colombia, Maryland, Virginia and West Virginia.

CHICAGO:
7358 South Pulaski Rd.
Chicago, IL 60629
Serves Illinois, Indiana, Michigan, Minnesota, Ohio, and Wisconsin.

ATLANTA:
1557 St. Joseph Ave.
East Point, GA 30344
Serves Alabama, Georgia, Florida, Kentucky, Mississippi, North Carolina, South Carolina, and Tennessee.

KANSAS CITY:
2306 East Bannister Rd.
Kansas City, MO 64131
Serves Iowa, Kansas, Missouri, and Nebraska

FORT WORTH:
4900 Hemphill St. (building address)
P.O. Box 6216 (mailing address)
Fort Worth, TX 76115
Serves Arkansas, Louisiana, New Mexico, Oklahoma, and Texas.

DENVER:
Building 48, Denver Federal Center
Denver, CO 80225
Serves Colorado, Montana, North Dakota, South Dakota, Utah, and Wyoming.

SAN FRANCISCO:
1000 Commodore Drive
San Bruno, CA 94066
Serves California except Southern California; Hawaii; Nevada except Clark County, and the Pacific Ocean area.

LOS ANGELES:
24000 Avila Rd.
Laguna Niguel, CA 92677
Serves Arizona; the Southern California counties of Imperial, Inyo, Kern, Los Angeles, Orange, Riverside, San Bernardino, San Diego, San Luis Obispo, Santa Barbara, and Ventura; and Clark County, Nevada.

SEATTLE:
6125 Sand Point Way, N.E.
Seattle, WA 98115
Serves Alaska, Idaho, Oregon, and Washington.

APPENDIX B

Naturalization Records in the Regional Archives Branches

Note: *One should write first to the Clerk of the Court to obtain the petition of declaration of intent number before writing to the regional archives branch. All inquiries should be addressed to the Chief, Archives Branch, Federal Archives and Records Center.*

380 Trapelo Rd.
Waltham, MA 021454

Federal court records for Massachusetts, Rhode Island, and Connecticut. Does have a name index to the naturalization records of the U.S. District Court and the U.S. Circuit Court for Massachusetts for the years 1790-1906.

Building 22—Military Ocean Terminal
Bayonne, NJ 07002

Federal court records for New York and New Jersey. Does have indexes and photocopies of naturalization records, 1792-1906.

5000 Wissahickon Ave.
Philadelphia, PA 19144

Federal court records for Pennsylvania, Delaware, Maryland, Virginia, and West Virginia.

7358 South Pulaski Rd.
Chicago, IL 60629

Federal court records for Ohio, Indiana, Illinois, Michigan, Wisconsin, and Minnesota. All Cook County, Illinois, naturalization records from 1871, whether county or federal in origin, are controlled by an index in the custody of the Immigration and Naturalization Service. Inquiries should be addressed to that agency, 219 South Dearborn St., Chicago, Illinois 60604.

2306 East Bannister Road
Kansas City, MO 64131

Federal court records for Southern Iowa, Kansas, Minnesota, and Missouri.

P.O. Box 6216
Fort Worth, TX 76115
Federal court records for Arkansas, Louisiana, Oklahoma, and Texas.

Building 48, Denver Federal Center
Denver, CO 80225
Federal court records for Colorado, Montana, North Dakota, South Dakota, Utah, and Wyoming.

24000 Avila Rd.
Laguna Niguel, CA 92677
Federal court records for Los Angeles and San Diego, California; Arizona; and San Diego County indexes and records of naturalization.

1000 Commodore Drive
San Bruno, CA 94066
Federal court records for San Francisco and Sacramento, California; Hawaii; Washoe and Churchill counties, Nevada.

6125 Sand Point Way, N.E.
Seattle, WA 98115
Federal court records for Washington and Montana; county naturalization records in Idaho and Alaska.

Appendix C

Sources of Vital Statistics *(Birth, Death, and Marriages)*

ALABAMA:
Bureau of Vital Statistics
State Department of Health
Montgomery, AL 36130
Births and deaths from 1908 on. Before that, county clerk's office. Marriages found in county clerk of probate court.

ALASKA:
Bureau of Vital Statistics
State Department of Health and Social Services
P.O. Box H 02G
Juneau, AK 99881
Births, deaths, marriages from 1913 on.

ARIZONA:
Bureau of Vital Statistics
Department of Health Services
P.O. Box 3887
Phoenix, AZ 85030
Births and deaths from 1909 on. Marriage records, clerk of superior court where license was issued.

ARKANSAS:
Bureau of Vital Statistics
State Health Department
4815 West Markham St.
Little Rock, AR 72201
Births and deaths from 1914, marriages from 1917.

CALIFORNIA:
State Registrar of Vital Statistics
304 S Street
Sacramento, CA 95814
Births, deaths, and marriages since 1905. Prior to 1905, county recorder and some health departments. All county clerks also have some marriage records.

COLORADO:
State Bureau of Vital Statistics
Denver, CO 80202

Births from 1910 and deaths from 1900 on. Before that, county registrars. Marriage records kept by county clerks.

CONNECTICUT:
State Department of Health Services
Vital Records Service
79 Elm Street
Hartford, CT 06116

Birth, death, and marriage records since 1897. Earlier records found in city or town clerk records.

DELAWARE:
Bureau of Vital Statistics
Jesse S. Cooper Memorial Bldg.
Dover, DE 19901

Births, death, marriages since 1913. Before that, the state archives Hall of Records, Dover, DE 19901.

DISTRICT OF COLUMBIA:
Bureau of Vital Statistics
Health Department
425 I Street, N.W. Room 3009
Washington, D.C. 20001

Births from 1874 on, deaths from 1855 on, except 1861 and 1862. Marriages are with the U.S. District Court Clerk, Fourth and E Streets, N.W. Washington, D.C. 20001.

FLORIDA:
Office of Vital Statistics
P.O. Box 210
Jacksonville, FL 32231

Births from 1865 to present, deaths from 1877 to present. Marriages from 1927 to present, earlier are found in county judge's office.

GEORGIA:
Vital Records Service, Room 217-H
47 Trinity Ave., S.W.
Atlanta, GA 30334

Births and deaths from 1919 to present. Marriages from 1952 to present. Earlier marriages may be found in county clerk or clerk of the ordinary court.

HAWAII:
Research and Statistics Office
State Department of Health
P.O. Box 3378
Honolulu, Hawaii 96801
Births, deaths, and marriage records from 1853 on.

IDAHO:
Bureau of Vital Statistics
State Department of Health and Welfare
Boise, ID 83720
Births and deaths from 1911, marriages since 1947, between 1907 and 1911, county recorder has records.

ILLINOIS:
Department of Public Health
535 W. Jefferson St.
Springfield, IL 67261
Births and deaths from 1916 on. Marriage records and early birth and death records are in county clerk's office.

INDIANA:
Indiana State Board of Health
1330 West Michigan St.
Indianapolis, IN 46206
Births from 1907, deaths from 1900. Before that, in the health department of county or occurrence. Marriages from 1958, before that in the court clerk of county of license issuance.

IOWA:
Division of Vital Records
Iowa State Department of Health
Lucas State Office Bldg.
Des Moines, IA 50319
Births from 1880, deaths from 1891, marriages from 1916. Before that, marriages are in county clerk's office.

KANSAS:
Bureau of Vital Statistics
6700 S. Topeka Ave.
Topeka, KS 66620
Births and deaths from 1911 on, marriages since 1913. Before that, marriages are in probate judge's court.

KENTUCKY:
Bureau of Vital Statistics
275 E. Main St.
Frankfort, KY 40601

Births and deaths from 1911, marriages since 1958. Prior to that, county clerk's office.

LOUISIANA:
Division of Vital Records
Department of Health and Human Resources
P.O. Box 60630
New Orleans, LA 70160

Births and deaths since 1914. Parish (county) clerks have early birth and death records and all marriage records.

MAINE:
Division of Vital Records
Human Services State House
Augusta, ME 04333

Births, deaths and marriages from 1892. Earlier, town clerks.

MARYLAND:
Division of Vital Records
Department of Health
201 W. Preston St.
Baltimore, MD 21203

Births and deaths, 1898 to present, marriages from 1951. Marriage records prior to that time can be found in office of the clerk of the circuit court.

MASSACHUSETTS
State Registrar of Vital Records
150 Tremont St., Room B-3
Boston, MA 02111

Birth, death, and marriage records since 1841. Before that, the city or town clerk's office, or State Archives, State House, Boston.

MICHIGAN:
Vital Records
State Department of Public Health
3500 North Logan St.
Lansing, MI 48909

Birth, death and marriage records from 1867, before that, the clerk of circuit court.

MINNESOTA:
Minnesota Department of Health
Birth and Death Records
717 Delaware St., S.E.
Minneapolis, MN 55440

Birth and death records from 1908, before that, birth, death and all marriage records are in the office of the clerks of the district courts in all counties.

MISSISSIPPI:
Vital Records
Mississippi State Board of Health
P.O. Box 1700
Jackson, MS 39215

Births and deaths since 1912, marriages and earlier births and deaths are kept by the circuit clerks .

MISSOURI:
Department of Social Services
Division of Health
P.O. Box 570
Jefferson City, MO 65102

Births and deaths from 1910, before that county clerk's office. Marriages from 1825, recorder of deeds office.

MONTANA:
Records and Statistics
Department of Health and Environmental Services
Capitol Station
Helena, Montana 59620

Birth and death records from 1907, earlier county clerk. Marriages, clerk of court where license was issued.

NEBRASKA:
Bureau of Vital Statistics
Department of Health
301 Centennial Mall South
Lincoln, NE 68509

Birth and death records since 1904, marriage records since 1909. Prior to those dates, the records are available at the office of the county clerk.

NEVADA:
State Department of Health
Division of Vital Statistics
Carson City, NV 89710

Births and deaths from 1911; earlier, county recorder. Marriages, at county recorder.

NEW HAMPSHIRE:
Bureau of Vital Statistics
Health and Welfare Bldg.
Hazen Drive
Concord, NH 03301

Births, deaths, and marriages from 1640, also in offices of town clerk.

NEW JERSEY:
State Bureau of Vital Statistics
Health Department,
CN 360
Trenton, NJ 08625

Births, deaths and marriage records from 1878 to present. Other marriage records at county clerk's office.

NEW MEXICO:
Vital Statistics Bureau
P.O. Box 968
Santa Fe, NM 87504

Birth and death notices from 1920, some delayed birth records from 1867. Marriage records at county clerk's office.

NEW YORK: (State)
Bureau of Vital Statistics
Department of Health
ESP Tower Bldg.
Albany, NY 12237

Births and deaths since 1880 and marriages from 1880, except for Albany, Buffalo, and Yonkers; for them, check with their city clerk or registrar of vital statistics.

NEW YORK: (City)
NYC Department of Health
125 Worth St.
New York City, NY 10013

Births from 1898 and deaths from 1920.

NY City Clerk
Chambers and Centre St.
New York, NY 10007
Marriage records from 1866.

NORTH CAROLINA:
Department of Human Resources
Division of Health Services
Vital Records Branch
P.O. Box 2091
Raleigh, NC 27602
Births from 1913 and deaths from 1930, earlier from State Archives. Some marriages from 1925, earlier from registrar of deeds.

NORTH DAKOTA:
Division of Vital Records
Department of Health
Bismarck, ND 58505
Births and deaths from 1893, marriages since 1925. Earlier marriages found in office of county judge.

OHIO:
Division of Vital Statistics
Department of Health, Room G-20
65 S. Front St.
Columbus, OH 43215
Births and deaths from 1908, marriages from 1949. Earlier for all three found in the county probate court of event.

OKLAHOMA:
Department of Health
Division of Vital Statistics
N.E. 10th and Stonewall
Oklahoma City, OK 73152
Births and deaths from 1908, marriages are at county clerk's office.

OREGON:
State Registrar
Board of Health Department
P.O. Box 116
Portland, OR 97207
Births and deaths since 1903, marriages since 1907. Earlier marriages may be found in county clerk's office.

PENNSYLVANIA:
Division of Vital Statistics
P.O. Box 1528
Newcastle, PA 16103

Births and deaths since 1906, before that, at the county clerk of occurrence. Marriage records are at county clerk.

RHODE ISLAND:
Division of Vital Statistics
State Department of Health, Room 101, Cannon Bldg.
75 Davis Street
Providence, RI 02908

Birth and death records are from 1853. Marriage records and earlier birth and death records are in town or city clerk's office.

SOUTH CAROLINA:
Division of Vital Records, Department of Health
2600 Bull Street
Columbia, SC 29201

Births and deaths from 1915, marriages from 1950. Marriages from 1911 at office of probate judge in county of event.

SOUTH DAKOTA:
Department of Health, Vital Records Program
Joe Foss Office Bldg.
Pierre, SD 57501

Births, deaths, and marriages from 1905. Earlier marriages at county clerk of occurrence.

TENNESSEE:
Division of Vital Records, Department of Health
Cordel Hull Bldg.
Nashville, TN 37219

Births and deaths from 1914, earlier from county of occurrence. Marriage records before 1945, from the county clerk, after that from the State Division of Vital Records.

TEXAS:
Bureau of Vital Statistics, Department of Health
1100 West 49th St.
Austin, TX 78756

Births and deaths, from 1903; earlier, county clerk's office. Marriages, county clerk's office of issuance of license.

UTAH:
Bureau of Health Statistics
Department of Health
150 West North Temple St.
Salt Lake City, UT 84110

Births and deaths since 1905. Marriage records are at the county clerk's office of issuance of license.

VERMONT:
Secretary of State
Vital Records
109 State St.
Montpelier, VT 05602

Birth, death, and marriage records from 1760 to 1955. From that time, the records are found at the state health department, 60 Main St., Burlington, VT 05402.

VIRGINIA:
Bureau of Vital Statistics and Health Services
P.O. Box 1000
Richmond, VA 23208

Birth, death, and marriages since 1853, except for the period from 1896 to 1912. For those dates check with the city or town health department for records.

WASHINGTON:
Department of Health
Bureau of Vital Statistics
P.O. Box 9709 ET-11
General Administration Bldg.
Olympia, WA 98504

Birth and death records since 1907, before that, in the office of the county auditor. Marriages are also at the county auditor of occurrence.

WEST VIRGINIA:
Division of Vital Statistics
Department of Health
State Office Bldg. No. 3
Charleston, WV 25305

Births and deaths from 1917, earlier from the county clerk. Marriages from 1921, earlier from the county clerk.

WISCONSIN:
Bureau of Health Statistics
P.O. Box 309
Madison, WI 53701
Births and deaths from 1860, marriages from 1835.

WYOMING:
Division of Vital Statistics
Health and Medical Services
Hathaway Bldg.
Cheyenne, WM 82002
Births and deaths from 1909; earlier, the county clerk of occurrence. Marriages are from 1941; earlier, county clerk's office.

Outside the U.S.

CANADA:
Public Archives of Canada:
395 Wellington Street
Ottawa, Ontario KIA ON3
Canada
Contains census records, military records, and immigration records. Births, deaths and marriages are found at individual provinces or territories.

MEXICO:
Archivo General de la Nación: (National Archives)
Palacio Nacional
México, 1 DF
Contains notorial records (legal records such as wills, deeds, land records, and letters of indebtedness). Since 1859 births, deaths, and marriages are at municipal level. Individual Catholic parishes have baptisms, marriages, and burial records also.

ENGLAND AND WALES:
General Register Office: St. Catherine's House
10 Kingsway
London WC2B 6JP, England
Contains births, marriages, and deaths from 1 July 1937.

Public Record Office: Chancery Lane
London WC2 1LR, England
Has census records from 1801, wills, and some church records.

SCOTLAND:
Register General: New Register House
Edinburgh, EH1 3YT
Scotland

Since 1855, births, deaths, and marriages, also census records from 1841.

Scottish Record Office: P.O. Box 36
H.M. General Register House
Edinburgh, EH1 3YT
Scotland

Has wills and land records (deeds, leases since early 17th century).

IRELAND:
Republic of Ireland (Eire)
The Public Record Office of Ireland: Four Courts
Dublin 7, Ireland

Has census records from 1821, wills, and some church records.

Office of the Registrar General: The Custom House
Dublin 1, Ireland

Contains births, marriages, and deaths from 1 January 1864.

Northern Ireland
Public Record Office of Northern Ireland: (PRONI)
66 Balmoral Avenue
Belfast BT9 6NY
Northern Ireland

Has some census records from 1821, but most lost in fire in 1922. Has births, marriage, and death records from 1864 up to 1922. Also has some wills, probate records, and church records.

Central Registry Office: Fermanagh House
Belfast BT2 8HX
Northern Ireland

Has vital records (births, deaths, and marriages) from 1922.

Bureau of Indian Affairs Area Offices

WASHINGTON D.C.
BIA Headquarters, Bureau of Indian Affairs
1849 C Street, N.W.
Washington, D.C. 20240
(202) 208-3711

ABERDEEN AREA OFFICE
Bureau of Indian Affairs
115 4th Avenue, S.E.
Aberdeen, SD 57401-4382
(605) 226-7343
Serves Nebraska, North Dakota, and South Dakota.

ALBUQUERQUE AREA OFFICE
Bureau of Indian Affairs
615 First Street, N.W.
Albuquerque, NM 87125-6567
(505) 766-3171
Serves Colorado and New Mexico.

ANADARKO AREA OFFICE
Bureau of Indian Affairs
WCD Office Complex
P.O. Box 368
Anadarko, OK 73005-0368
(405) 247-6673
Serves Kansas and Western Oklahoma.

BILLINGS AREA OFFICE
Bureau of Indian Affairs
316 North 26th Street
Billings, MT 59101-1397
(406) 657-6315
Serves Montana and Wyoming.

EASTERN AREA OFFICE
Bureau of Indian Affairs
3701 North Fairfax Drive
Suite 260
Arlington, VA 22203
(703) 235-2571
Serves New York, Maine, Louisiana, Florida, North Carolina, Mississippi, Connecticut, and Rhode Island.

JUNEAU AREA OFFICE
Bureau of Indian Affairs
Federal Building
P.O. Box 3-8000
Juneau, AK 99802-1219
(907) 586-7177
Serves Alaska.

MINNEAPOLIS AREA OFFICE
Bureau of Indian Affairs
331 Second Avenue South
Minneapolis, MN 55401-2241
(612) 373-1000
Serves Minnesota, Iowa, Michigan, and Wisconsin

MUSKOGEE AREA OFFICE
Bureau of Indian Affairs
5th and West Okmulgee Streets
Muskogee, OK 74401-4898
(918) 687-2296
Serves Eastern Oklahoma.

NAVAJO AREA OFFICE
P.O. Box M, Box 1060
Gallup, NM 87305-1060
(505) 863-9501
Serves Navajo Reservation only, Arizona, Utah, and New Mexico.

PHOENIX AREA OFFICE
Bureau of Indian Affairs
1 North First Street
Phoenix, AZ 85001-0010
(602) 379-6600
Serves Arizona, Nevada, Utah, and Idaho.

PORTLAND AREA OFFICE
Bureau of Indian Affairs
911 NE 11th Avenue
Portland, OR 97232-4169
(503) 231-6702

Serves Oregon, Washington, and Idaho.

SACRAMENTO AREA OFFICE
Federal Office Building
2800 Cottage Way
Sacramento, CA 95825-1884
(916) 978-4691

Serves California.

IMMIGRANTS:

Baxter, Angus. *In Search of Your British and Irish Roots.* New York, 1982.

___. *In Search of Your European Roots.* Baltimore, Maryland, 1986.

Cooke, Alistair. *Alistair Cooke's America.* New York, 1973.

Hamilton-Edwards, Gerald. *In Search of Scottish Ancestors.* Baltimore, Maryland, 1986.

___. *Tracing Your British Ancestors.* New York, 1967.

The National Geographic Book Service. *We, Americans.* Washington, D.C., 1975.

Morison, Samuel Eliot. *The Oxford History of the American People.* New York, 1965.

Smith, Jessie Carney, Editor. *Ethnic Genealogy, A Research Guide.* Westport, Connecticut, 1983.

BLACKS:

Abajian, James de T. *Blacks in Selected Newspapers, Censuses and Sources: An Index to Names and Subjects.* Boston, Massachusetts, 1976.

Schatz, Walter, Editor. *The Directory of Afro-American Resources.* New York, 1970.

Haley, Alex. *Roots.* Garden City, New York, 1976.

Nash, Gary B. *Red, White and Black.* Englewood Cliffs, New Jersey, 1974.

Rose, James and Eicholz, Alice. *Black Genesis.* Detroit, Michigan, 1978.

Sowell, Thomas. *Ethnic America.* New York, 1981.

Walker, James D. *Black Genealogy: How to Begin.* Athens University of Georgia, Center for Continuing Education, 1977.

INDIANS:

Carpenter, Cecelia S. *How to Research American Indian Blood Lines.* Orting, Washington, 1987.

Debo, Angie. *A History of Indians in the United States.* Norman, Oklahoma, 1972.

Dillon, Richard H. *Indian Wars.* New York, 1984.

Hill, Edward. *Guide to Records in the National Archives of the United States Relating to American Indians.* Washington, D.C., 1981.

Hodge, Frederick Webb. *The Handbook of American Indians North of Mexico.* New York, 1959.

Josephy, Alvin, Jr. *The Indian Heritage of America.* New York, 1969.

Kirkham, E. Kay. *Our Native Americans and Their Records of Genealogical Value.* Vol. I and II. Logan, Utah, 1980 and 1984.

Lavender, David. *The Great West.* New York, 1982.

Locke, Raymond Friday, Editor. *The American Indian.* New York, 1970.

Marquis, Arnold. *A Guide to American Indians.* Norman, Oklahoma, 1974.

Meggers, Betty J. *Prehistoric America.* Chicago, Illinois, 1972.

National Geographic Society. *The World of the American Indians.* Washington, D.C., 1974.

Swanton, John R. *Indian Tribes of North America.* Washington, D.C., 1952.

U.S. Department of the Interior. *American Indians Today.* Washington, D.C., 1991.

HERALDRY:

Child, Heather. *Heraldic Design.* London and Southhampton, 1965.

Franklyn, Julian. *Heraldry.* Cranbury, New Jersey, 1968.

Scott-Giles, C.W. and Brooke-Little, J.P. *Boutell's Heraldry.* London, 1973.

COMPUTER GENEALOGY:

Pense, Richard A., Editor. *Computer Genealogy: A Guide to Research Through High Technology.* Salt Lake City, Utah, 1991.

Ancestry Publishing. *Genealogical Computing.* Vol. 8, No. 4. Salt Lake City, Utah, 1989.

Andreck, Paul A. and Pence, Richard A. *Computer Genealogy.* Salt Lake City, Utah, 1985.

Arnold, David. *Getting Started With the IBM PC and XT.* New York, 1984.

Garetz, Mark. *Bits, Bytes and Buzzwords.* Beaverton, Oregon, 1983.

Posey, Joanna D. *Tracing Your Roots by Computer.* Orem, Utah, 1985.

Poynter, Dan. *Computer Selection Guide.* Santa Barbara, California, 1983.

GENERAL REFERENCE:

Beard, Timothy Field and Demong, Denise. *How to Find Your Family Roots.* New York, 1977.

Doane, Gilbert H. and Bell, James B. *Searching for Your Ancestors.* Minneapolis, Minnesota, 1980.

Everton, George B., Sr., Editor. *The Handy Book for Genealogists.* Logan, Utah, 1981.

Filby, William P. and Meyers, Mary K., Editors. *A Guide to Published Arrival Records of About 500,000 Passengers Who Came to America and Canada in the Seventeenth, Eighteenth and Nineteenth Centuries.* 3 Vol. Detroit, Michigan, 1983.

Greenwood, Val D. *The Researcher's Guide to American Genealogy.* Baltimore, Maryland, 1978.

Helmbold, Wilbur R. *Tracing Your Ancestry.* Birmington, Alabama, 1976.

Hotton, John Camden. *The Original Lists of Persons of Quality.* New York, 1874.

Immigrant Information, Inc. *The Morton Allan Directory of European Passenger Steamship Arrivals.* New York, 1979.

Kirkham E. Kay. *Simplified Genealogy for Americans.* Salt Lake City, Utah, 1968.

Lancour, Harold. *A Bibliography of Ship Passenger Lists, 1538-1825.* New York, 1963.

National Archives Trust Fund Board. *Genealogical Research in the National Archives.* Washington, D.C., 1983.

Stryker-Rodda, Harriet. *How to Climb Your Family Tree.* Baltimore, Maryland, 1983.

Westin, Jeanne Eddy. *Finding Your Roots.* Los Angeles, California, 1977.

Williams, Ethel W. *Know Your Ancestors.* Rutland, Vermont, 1969.

U.S. Department of Health and Human Services. *Where to Write for Vital Records.* Hyattsville, Maryland, 1984.

Index

Please send me

Searching for Lost Ancestors

copies @ $10.95 each	=	
California sales tax (7.75%) (Calif. residents only)	=	
Shipping ($2.00 per order)	=	$2.00
TOTAL	=	

Name

Address

City

State Zip

❑ My check is enclosed

Return to

DONALD UNDERWOOD

12001 Prospect Hill Drive

Gold River, CA 95670